BERNARD BERENSON

Sketch for a Self-Portrait

PANTHEON

333 Sixth Avenue, New York 14, N. Y.

Manufactured in U.S.A.
Printed by Belgrave Press, Inc., New York

ACKNOWLEDGMENTS

The Author and his Publishers are indebted to Sir Edward Marsh and to Eyre & Spottiswoode (Publishers) Ltd., for permission to include in this book part of Sir Edward's translation of La Fontaine's *Invocation*.

With the exception of the frontispiece and the portrait of Bernard Berenson as a student in Harvard, all photographs are by LIFE photographer Dmitri Kessel.

IN MEMORY OF MY WIFE AND
FIFTY YEARS OF COMPANIONSHIP

PREFACE

Can any mortal portray himself with words, as perhaps he can with chalk or paint? The limner has something relatively definite before him as he looks into the glass and sees himself mirrored there. I doubt the representative accuracy of even such an image. But words! What can they do but apply this or that epithet, this or that descriptive, interpretative, evocative phrase; recount that anecdote, or that praiseworthy, or blameworthy deed? A gifted verbal artist may convey some coherent idea of a person he attempts to portray, but not likely an objective one.

No matter what your talent as an author, where are you to catch yourself *en flagrant délit* of being yourself, yours individually, privately, yet representative and consistent?

Be that as it may be, I for one am not sure just which of my so many selves, at different moments of my life, would represent me most faithfully. I can only attempt to offer glimpses into my present self or selves, those glimpses which in recent years have flashed more recurrently through my mind. Indeed the reader may notice that in this volume, as well as in the *Diary* which will follow it and in my book on *Aesthetics and History in the Visual Arts,* there is a tendency for certain ideas, certain subjects, certain preoccupations to appear again and again as the wooden horses in a merry-go-round.

So I have tried to jot down some glimpses into that chaos and to dip into that stream of consciousness we are accustomed to call self. They are few, for most whirl or flow away. And those few are handed over freed from impurities as it were, and too deodorized by our invincible and irremediable self-regard, to have more value than that of meteoric flashes in a dark sky. *Self-glimpses* might be the best title for this book, or better still *Self-dippings,* if I could endure the combination of syllables. *Glimpses into Self* or *Dippings into Self* sounds awkward and affected. So unless my publisher hits upon a better title, let it be *Sketch for a Self-portrait.*

CASA AL DONO, VALLOMBROSA.
September 20th, 1945

PART ONE

I

OFTEN I feel like a cow with sagging udders lowing for calf or milkmaid to relieve her. Or like a plant that oozes ink instead of syrup or resin and craves to have it properly drawn off. Wherefore I enjoy companionship that draws one out to talk, and correspondents who stimulate one to write. To the well disposed there is nothing more effective for either satisfaction than blank paper. When one's own mental state refuses to become creative, remains obstinately impotent, then the ink that is in me searches an outlet and finds it in letter-writing.

Thus on travel, although so busy sight-seeing and losing so much time in being carried from place to place, I find leisure for letters. There are no friends to draw me out in talk and no preoccupations with authorship to absorb me.

A pity that talk is not self-registering! Hundreds and hundreds, thousands and thousands of yards of paper would preserve my bright sayings, my provoking epithets, my wit, my wisdom, my learning—in short the outpourings of my heart and mind and spirit. I never got over the wonder I used to feel as a little boy that potatoes could fill a sack, water a pail, smoke a room, but words left every recipient empty no matter how much you talked into it. The more the pity, for I was born to talk and not to write and, worse still, to converse rather than to talk and then only with stimulating interlocutors. Oddly enough, these are not necessarily friends. They may be total strangers or the merest acquaintances. They must, however, have the eagerness, the curiosity, the responsiveness, to start my tongue wagging and, I must add unblushingly, wagging to a purpose. I am as easily put off as mediumistic performers by the presence of doubters. My audience must believe and accept, not necessarily what I say, but me as a talker worth their while.

Oftener than not, the most stimulating listeners would not be able to relate (or give account of) what I said, for the simple reason that they retained but the vaguest and most confused notion of what I was driving at, having enough brains to feel fascinated but not enough to understand. So we prefer the cosy comfort and lounging ease of talk with inferiors to the challenging and fatiguing society of superiors or even equals.

Mrs. Winthrop Chanler tells in her memoirs how marvellously Henry Adams talked to one of her daughters on a late evening, when the young woman and he were alone. When he stopped she looked up in ecstasy, transfigured. "Do you know, my child, why I talked? I was confident you would not understand a word of what I was saying."

Henry Adams on that occasion had found an innocent ear; he had reached the stage when one no longer itches to communicate, impart and persuade, but still feels the need of a "receiver" for the soliloquy with which head and heart are bursting. I have not got so far. I delight in the glowing sympathy of the audience but I require it to participate and stimulate. I expect it to crank me up with inspiring questions when I seem to be running short, or even, as is more apt to be the case, with some idiotic remark that has a metaphysical lining or sting.

This kind of audience will not be recruited among hard-boiled, too grown-up adults. We shall find it rather among individuals, of whatever age or sex, who remain adolescent-minded to the end. Women not overburdened with family, or philanthropy, or politics. Men in diplomacy, in business and in professions that leave them some leisure of mind. Men and women, they must be sufficiently acquainted with things of the spirit as well as with things of the world, to crave not only to know more but also to understand better, to thirst for clarification not less than for information.

They will be women more often than men, for women do not compete in the same field. If the desire for possession does not intervene, men and women can be so much better friends than men with men and women with women, subject as we are to jealousy, envy, and spite that, sugar it over as you will, accompany even the most civilized competitiveness.

So my kind of person turns to women, surrounds himself with women, appeals to women, not in the first place and perhaps not at all for reasons of sex, no matter how deodorized, alembicated and transubstantiated, but for the one deciding reason that women, especially certain society women, are more receptive, more appreciative and consequently more stimulating. Let colleagues, equals and superiors jeer as they please, but when youth is well over, colleagues seldom draw each other out. They are more likely to freeze the tender shoots of each other's tentativeness, suggestiveness and wistfulness with the hard frost of their logic and scholarship, the instruments of their instinctive pugnacity. They tend to inhibit rather than to encourage talk except as a hard competition in a verbal prize-fight.

To confess to preferring the society of the adolescent-minded may be to write oneself down as second- or even third-rate, compared with the stags who engage their tangled horns of learning in sublime and intellectual contest.

We second- and third-rate folk can find comfort in Socrates, in Plato and in many other thinkers, men of science and men of letters, who lived before or after the monastic period—a period with traditions that have left an impress upon universities until only the other day. They frequented the adolescent-minded by choice, and seldom the overmature. With the last they joined in controversy; in social intercourse perhaps never.

But present conditions crab and confine my social radiation to a minimum. Living among a people at war, as the citizen of a non-belligerent country with opposed sympathies, and residing in a town like Florence, renowned for its clamorous patriotism, it is quite natural that I see few Italians. Foreigners do not come. Dear English and American friends who used to stay are not to be expected. Not only that it is almost impossible to keep up correspondence with them. Even if letters do succeed in getting through, they have to pass censorship after censorship and one is reduced to the epistolary style of the humble and untutored who write that they are well and hope that you too are well. The ink that was in me used to flow out as from the rivers of Paradise to friends not only in America, but in England, in France, in *Germania*. Now that I cannot shed it, I suffer almost as from a physical stoppage. In normal times, when in my home and library and study, I write or am preoccupied with the idea of composing for print which takes up my pen to a great extent. But now anxieties, excitements, despondencies, speculations related to the war skim one's energies to such a degree that there is little left over wherewith to concentrate on abstract and impersonal subjects.

And yet the itch to write is strong enough to make me uncomfortable when I pass a day *sine linea*—without putting down something in black and white.

2

A friend who is staying here came to my study yesterday evening for a confidential chat. Talking of her husband she told me he had not changed in his reactions, in his attitudes toward the world, toward society, toward the family, in twenty-two years. In short, and to use my own language, he was as grown-up twenty-two years ago as he has been since, as hard boiled. As this friend and her husband are both Neapolitans I heard myself say what a pity it was that adults could not liquefy like the blood of Saint Januarius.

In this instance there was a fraction of a second's awareness in me of what I was going to say. Usually images, metaphors, comparisons, slip from my tongue before I become aware of what I am going to say.

If at my age the winged words still come to the lips it is not so with names. Names already on the tip of the tongue instead of passing the teeth dart back like lizards. I used to have a fair memory for names and even for words. I was particularly good at recalling every substantive connected with my job. Now the small fry glide away like minnows into the waters of Lethe. Yet in some mysterious way one's wish does often get them back, when one's will has given up trying.

Memory is curious, capricious, incalculable, inexplicable, like all other realities. What is it? Is it a thread? No, rather a nerve rivulet conveying what is left over of a vital experience from somewhere in the past to the present instant. The loss of memory begins with attenuating this flow until it almost stops. Thereupon this something that hitherto had a warmth, as if it were an extension, no matter how remote, of our blood-stream, ceases to be part of us, never to be reintegrated with ourselves, even if we do recapture it and save it for mere use. Strange things happen to me in my seventy-sixth year. So much of what only the other day seemed part and parcel of my mental furniture has faded and vanished before I have perceived it. Could I have retained it with a timely effort? I could not have believed that I would forget my Greek irregular verbs, the dates of the kings of England, the succession of our presidents, the rivers, the capitals, the boundaries of our individual states. I find I am forgetting them or have lost them already. Huge lumps of memory break away and melt into oblivion. Why? How? Is memory a tablet, a palimpsest, criss-crossed and written over and over, till no ground is visible through a tangle of inextricable confusion? Is that why we cease to retain easily and then not at all after a certain age, and why the tablet breaks off at the edges and cracks in the middle? Again, memory seems to act as if it consisted of a pile of photographic negatives. During our best years these negatives present themselves unbidden when wanted. Now they ignore my orders. What has happened? Have they failed in energy and readiness, have they faded, or is it my ego that can no longer command their obedience?

I wonder sometimes whether memory is not the core of one's own feeling of identity. If a cut is made in the stream of memory, the part that flows away ceases to be us. If this or that is dipped up in buckets and recognized as having formerly been us, it now is no more us than the hair and nails or even meaner products of the body that we have shed. Life is short enough, yet few retain a memory continuous from their early childhood to the present minute. Most of us have but a shapeless sense of the past and few moments retain their vital contact with us, these few getting rarer and dimmer the nearer they retreat toward boyhood and childhood. When we succeed in calling up this or that episode of childhood, boyhood, youth, we are indifferent, feel no responsibility, no sense that it was ourselves that did or were done to.

Memory may be the core of the sense of one's own personality, but this sense has much besides, many threads of various tissues and colours are wound round this core. Of this more at some other time perhaps. Just now I want to ask what becomes of immortality if memory is so fragile, so uncertain, so wavering, so feeble that it cannot successfully and uninterruptedly stretch across the brief space of mortal life. It would have to be endowed with miraculous powers to preserve for thousands and ever more thousands of years, world without end, a feeling of being still the same that one was for some paltry decades here below. For all we know, each of us, like the Buddha, has already had countless lives, millions and millions of lives, been everything from a mouse to a Messiah, from a squirrel to a Shakespeare, from a goat to a god. What boots it, considering we have no complete recollection of even one life! We shall scarcely take the evidence of self-adulating ladies of fashion who say that they have been Catherine the Great and before that Marie Stuart and earlier still Cleopatra. Nor can we be too much impressed by the anecdote that Pythagoras, seeing spear and shield hung up as trophies in a temple, recognized them as having belonged to him when in a former life he was the hero Euphorbus to whom they were dedicated. Comfort is offered by the beliefs current in certain West-Eastern circles that some day, at the end of time, in a flash, memory will recapture all one's multitude of lives. What cold comfort, colder than any point to which interstellar cold can sink.

3

There may be an immortal life for each of us, nay for every entity that ever has had life, but to finite minds like mine its ways and means as a condition of existence are inconceivable. Inconceivable unless indeed, as mystics tell us, we are to live after this mortal life in God, without memory, without individuality and without an identity of our own.

Were it realizable it would not be undesirable. As I look back on fully seventy years of awareness and recall the moments of greatest happiness, they were, for the most part, moments when I lost myself all but completely in some instant of perfect harmony. In consciousness this was due not to me but to the not-me, of which I was scarcely more than the subject in the grammatical sense.

In childhood and boyhood this ecstasy overtook me when I was happy out of doors. Was I five or six? Certainly not seven. It was a morning in early summer. A silver haze shimmered and trembled over the lime trees. The air was laden with their fragrance. The temperature was like a caress. I remember—I need not recall—that I climbed up a tree stump and felt suddenly immersed in Itness. I did not call it by that name. I had no need for words. It and I were one.

In the language of Thomas Traherne:

> "The corn was orient and immortal wheat, which never should be reaped, nor was ever sown, I thought it had stood from everlasting to everlasting. The dusk and the stones of the street were as precious as gold: the gates were at first the end of the world. The green trees when I saw them first through one of the gates transported and ravished me, their sweetness and unusual beauty made my heart to leap and almost mad with ecstasy . . . Eternity was manifest in the light of the day and

> something infinite behind everything appeared, which tallied with my expectations and moved my desire. The city seemed to stand in Eden and to be built in Heaven . . . the skies were mine and so were the sun and moon and stars, and all the world was mine and I the only spectator and enjoyer of it."

A revelation, a vision, a psychological equipoise, what you will, this experience has furnished me with a touchstone. It has remained for seven decades the goal of my yearning, my longing, my desire. Not always alas! but often enough in moments when passion, or ambition, or self-righteousness would have had their way with me, the feeling of that moment at the dawn of my conscious life would present itself and like a guardian angel remind me that IT was my goal and that IT was my only real happiness.

When I had learned to read and was already a boy, I identified myself with the heroes of the Old Testament, with the landscapes and characters in Jacob Abbot's *Franconia Stories,* with Robin Hood, with the Greek myths so charmingly New-Englandized by Hawthorne, then with the amphibious youngsters of Oliver Optic, Elijah Kellogg, Mayne Reid, and, of course, with Robinson Crusoe. I wonder who still reads any of them, excepting always the unfading *Robinson Crusoe,* and how many survive to recall them! I lived myself into all of them to the point of self-effacement. Surely most children are like that. I have retained that faculty through the years and can still melt into a good story, into its characters, its events, its tempo, to such a degree that my diaphragm loses its flexibility. Seldom can I take up an exciting narrative without being drawn on to finish it at a sitting, or rather at a lying down, even if it takes all night.

Later, after puberty, when love began to glow within me but for years remained unmixed with lust, my yearnings and longings were for a mystic being in youthful female shape with whom I could aspire to unite myself. And since then every time I was really in love to the degree of obsession, what I wanted was only to become one with the woman of my love, nay—to be absorbed by her, to end in her.

Through my whole mature life and increasingly with the piling up of the years, I have never enjoyed to the utmost a work of art of any kind, whether verbal, musical or visual, never enjoyed a landscape, without sinking my identity into that work of art, without becoming it, although, as in certain pictures and drawings of the sixteenth and seventeenth centuries we see tucked into a corner a tiny figure of the artist at work, so a minuscular observer is always there, watching, noting, appreciating, estimating, judging, always there in moments of utmost sensual and spiritual ecstasy and feeling with the rest, but still there.

Now I am in the decline of my eighth decade and live so much more in the people, the books, the works of art, the landscape than in my own skin, that of self, except as this wee homunculus of a perceiving subject, little is left over. A complete life may be one ending in so full an identification with the not-self that there is no self left to die.

This self—what is it? For about seventy years I have been asking that question. Can one frame an idea of one's own personality, map it out, make a picture of it that is in any measure convincing to an inquiring and fairly honest mind? In my case it has not been possible. I know what people think of me, favourably and unfavourably, and I have a sense of what composite image of me ends by taking shape in the minds of acquaintances. In my own mind and heart there is little correspondence with this image, although I have learned to accept it as that in me, to which others approach as to a treaty-port in old China or Japan. To myself I am an energy of a given force of radiation, and of a certain power of resistance; and I seem to be the same in these respects that I remember being when I completed my sixth year. I wonder whether this energy would not have been as effective in verse, in fiction, in history or—although less likely—in teaching or perchance in public life as it has been in the field that accident rather than an invincible tropism made me take. Outwardly as an "author," a jurist, a professor, a critic of events, I might have been a different person, but within I should be the same. Of course the stream of energy cannot help being affected by what it flows through, although nothing like so much as a river by its banks and affluences.

I seem to react in the same way now, and at the same pace, and to suffer the same kind of repulsion and attraction that I did at seven. Poor rhetorician that I am, yet I could expiate at length on this theme and enliven it with many bright anecdotes. There is no need. I do not mean to say that after so long a run, now approaching the infinite sea, I have retained the entire quality of my earliest years. In old age the primal energy not only approaches exhaustion but gets clogged, grows uncertain, is slowed up by all the sediments, salts and impurities that it has received and carried along. In essence I remain the same that I was at the dawn of my awareness.

Why should we not feel continuous identity within, seeing that from without we are taken for the same through all the ages? Any action, any course of conduct disapproved by the society surrounding us, is for ever held up to our faces like the gory head of a murdered man. Proust wants us to believe that in his Parisian world it was not so: that no matter what a person's past had been, how notorious, how shoddy, how criminal, after ten or twenty years this person would be received in the best company along with the most deserving. That may have been so in the ultra-fashionable Paris that Montesquiou displayed to Proust and that Proust worked up for our delectation. In the more responsible world it is not so. The extreme instance is the charge brought again and again in the Middle Ages that a certain wicked ruler showed his propensities in earliest infancy by fouling his baptismal font. A stronger conviction regarding the individual's essential sameness from cradle to grave could scarcely be entertained.

In the usual sense of the word "self" I feel as if I was never the same but—more than Hadrian's *animula vagula blandula*—a fluctuating, wavering, flickering something that is given momentary shape by what resistance it encounters in events, or more definitely in persons. Events cheer or depress me, but unfriendly persons often, if not always, make of me in my own awareness a creature nearer to their idea of me than to my own notion of myself, a person I dislike almost as much as they do. Another reason, by the way, why we self-indulgent individuals, too ease-loving to enjoy hard opposition and fierce logomachias, prefer softer company, ready to accept us at a valuation on the sunny side of our own fundamentally self-depreciating one, thereby increasing rather than diminishing our so easily deflated self-confidence.

4

Few experiences are more annoying than a first meeting that does not come off. It leaves one exasperated, skinned, and skinned roughly, suspecting it is one's own fault and wishing it had never taken place. I seldom get over such a failure. Only once did a rasping encounter that left me as if I had fought for hours through nettles and brambles with stinging buzzing flies tormenting and a blazing sun to parch one, only once did I get over such an introduction. And that was due to a ruse. It happened in this way.

Years ago, years before the last war, our neighbour Henry Y. Cannon invited me to meet Mr. and Mrs. Wharton. I had heard of her as well as read her and looked forward to the meeting with curiosity, expectation and hope. Placed next to her I tried in vain to get some human or even passably polite word out of her. She sniffed, she sneered, she jeered, she lost no occasion for putting in the wounding word, the venomous phrase. She left me exasperated and ashamed of my exasperation. I vowed never to see her again and no doubt reiterated this vow whenever her name came up among common friends.

Some years later in Paris, where I was seeing Henry Adams frequently, he invited me to dine with him one evening at Voisin's. I arrived and instead of finding him at his usual table on the ground floor I was led upstairs. It was in July. The room seemed full of acquaintances, but there was not enough daylight left to make out just who they were. Adams led me up to a lady who was seated by a window. She had a black lace veil over her face. I had no idea who she was. Her voice was pleasant. We fell into talk which got to interest me more and more. We seemed to share the same loves and hates in the realm of art. We agreed about the people whose names came up. I was wondering more and more who this delightful woman could be. Not a newcomer, surely. She was far too much in it for that. American no doubt but a foreign resident. It never occurred to me that she was what the electric light presently revealed, Edith Wharton.

She at once became a friend—a friend whose friendship soon got to be one of the most satisfactory of all my human relations. No devoted sister could have been more concerned for my comfort, more eager for my happiness. As an elder sister she never hesitated to reprove and advise, and for that I loved her. Yet all of a sudden she would begin to praise, to express her desire for the company of this or that person well known to her as being to me of unpleasant association.

One of these, peculiarly obnoxious, was notorious for his much trumpeted hate of Richard Wagner, Arthur Balfour and myself. I should have been flattered to make a third in such a trinity. Unfortunately Wagner was beyond his darts and Balfour beyond his reach, so I was left exposed to his slings and arrows. Edith Wharton knew this; and yet a naughty imp possessed her to tear the skin off a sore not yet healed over.

I have had another friend who was blessed with a most peculiar gift. No master of jiujitsu knew the sensitively weak spots of his opponent better than this friend understood where he could get me on the raw. He seldom failed to use this knowledge. He would praise other people, people I had no use for, in a provoking way as if they and not I were worthy of praise, deserving of success and popularity. In the course of nearly fifty years I should have got used to this naughtiness or nastiness. I never did, much as I argued with myself.

5

To return from my digression upon digression to what I was trying to say about the consciousness of self, I wish I could have some image, a coherent image of my personality with a definite shape and clear outlines. It is hard enough to know how one looks, impossible to know what one is. We are left to infer it from what people say about us and what we accept, reject, repel and controvert in what we heard about ourselves. We cannot even get a notion remotely parallel to what we acquire by staring into a mirror. That is little enough, for we gaze fixedly, we pose, we search and ask, "Is that me?" or, "Is it that or that?"; and when it happens once in a blue moon that we look into a mirror unexpectedly we seldom recognize the image there appearing as a reflection of ourselves. Yet how definite is this corporeal shape compared with any sense of one's entire personality, so uncharted, of such wavering outlines, of such uncertain heights and depths!

If our own looks as seen by others are little known to us, and our own notion of what we look like remains vague and subject to "wishful" imagining, our voices we are even less acquainted with. I remember speaking into a contraption that registered a sentence or two and in a minute the sound of the words came back to me. It had no relation as to tone pitch and quality with what I had just heard myself pronounce. And I remember that when Barrett Wendell heard the record of his own high-pitched voice, in see-sawing rhythm making it seem as if he spoke with "an English accent," he cried out, "The man with that voice should have his head cut off."

Except as an energy with attractions and repulsions that have undergone little change since earliest boyhood I have but an analytical acquaintance with myself. This leads to much that is distressing of which I am not yet prepared to speak, for as Heinrich Homberger says, "How frank we should be if we were as sure of being believed when we detailed our qualities as when we confess our faults." There is one particular source of torment due to a double dose of Hebraism, an original Jewish one and, piled tower-high above it, a New England puritan one.

It was my ideal to be unselfish and my duty to strive might and main to attain it. Do what I would, I never could feel it. My loves, affections and friendships and the conduct and actions seeming to result from them, I could not help tracking down to some motive of self-interest, self-indulgence or self-satisfaction. Love of women stripped of coatings, stood naked in its impersonal indifference to its object so long as that object complied with the demands made upon it. True, the object had to be of a certain kind and quality, but otherwise not individualized. It was not the unique being of my dreams, unparalleled in past, present and future, and utterly irreplaceable. With a little shifting of attention, a little steering of desire, any female of a given category would do as well. And, amazing no less than horrifying, the conclusion that her interests, her wishes, her private tropism had so little place in my thoughts.

I am affectionate and caressing by nature. It is selfish of me to indulge in these propensities. I feel baffled, frustrated, "inhibited," when the person or group I am with thwarts my impulse to embrace them in the radiance of my goodwill. It costs me dear to be chilly and stand-offish, for that calls out the same from others, which to me is intolerable. I have to run away or to make efforts, exaggerated and most likely out of place, to reconcile them, to win them over, to see them smile, in short to produce a genial atmosphere between us. So great is my dread of unbroken ice between others and myself that on the slightest provocation I avoid meeting people.

I cannot even now bear up against the suspicion that I am being taken at a value too remote from the one I am disposed to give myself. Let me cite two extreme instances of what I mean. The first is that the least contact with police authority, declared or no matter how delicately disguised, makes me feel, as Edith Wharton used to say of herself in the same case, a *rescapé de justice*—a recaptured criminal. I have never been able to make friends or even to be at ease with anyone wielding a particle of such authority. The second instance is of a different sort. In my thirties I enjoyed the conversation of a brilliant and intellectual acquaintance. One day he

had the candour to say that when he heard others talk, his chief interest was in the fallacies of logic they were committing. Circumstances separated us, but had they not, I doubt whether I could have talked to him again freely.

Friendship would seem to be the realm of disinterestedness. I have seldom or ever asked of a friend to intercede on my behalf or to procure me a material advantage. On the contrary I have deliberately and scrupulously avoided deriving benefit from friends, except the enjoyment of their society and the satisfaction of feeling that they were enjoying mine. Yet not so unselfish after all. Should they turn away or get duller and duller, the friendship would not survive.

For love, affection, friendship, are based on good behaviour, as indeed are all human relations, even the most impersonally official ones. Worse still, convenience and comfort play their part. We shun the friend who has turned sour or is loosing his mind. We avoid those who have got too indigent to keep up an appearance of reciprocal services. In the end we behave like the Spartans who expelled the citizen who could no longer contribute his share to the common mess of black broth.

So I cannot rid myself of the harassing feeling that I am at best but a refined and affectionate cannibal, like Herman Melville's South Sea friends. I try to comfort myself, though with no success, by assuming a difference between the unavoidable selfishness without which animal life could not continue, between the impenetrable solipsistic fog which prevents me from descrying anything wholly unselfish in any feeling or conduct of mine, and piggishness in small matters and cannibalism in greater ones. But I must define what I mean by cannibalism. I mean the use of anything alive, especially of our own species, and particularly any member of our own culture group, solely for our own supposed advantage, with no regard for their private interest and the common good of us all.

And yet I cannot recall being accused by others of inordinate selfishness. I have not been, as husbands go, a bad husband. I have seldom done anything without considering how it would affect my wife. Impulse carried me away a number of times but I was never unaware of what I was doing. Awareness tended to keep me straight. Likewise with friends. It has taken me a long time in each case to recognize that a friend had ceased to be a friend and changed first into an enemy-friend, and then into a person better avoided. Nor can I recall going back on a woman except one. Her I discovered using me as a laboratory specimen for experiments that I will not name. Objectively speaking, there is thus no ground for regarding myself as doing everything from a selfish motive. An illusion, no doubt, yet one that makes me sceptical even about my loyalty. I am too ready to question whether I am loyal for any deeper motive than that furnished by inertia, habit and self-indulgent sentimentality.

It is hard to reason myself out of the fear that I am merely an affectionate, caressing creature, satisfying a need almost physiological, rather than a person with a heart. I do not trust affectionateness any more than amorousness, which in fact it replaces when the other is congenitally feeble or enfeebled by age. Its most extravagant manifestations are among childless women, caressing, fondling, living for their lapdogs, but easily replacing them when they die. The fussiest exhibitions of this heartlessness are given by women who carry on a cruel war against a poor carter who has not been as considerate of his beast of burden as they would be to a pet; or who take a malignant dislike to an acquaintance who has clumsily trod on their spaniel's tail. I confess to a certain sympathy with the Neapolitan peasant who answers the protestations of the Anglo-Saxon spinster against his presumed unkindness to his beast with *"Non è cristiano"*—He is not a human being. I share the reluctance of Holy Church to give its blessing to societies for the protection of animals. But to return to affectionateness: selfish and cruelly indifferent men and women who would not lift a finger to help or comfort an acquaintance not present would spare no trouble, no expense, to procure for themselves the pleasure of that person's high spirits and jollity for so long as he was with them.

In every matter of personal concern I tend to put first the most interested, the most materialistic reason; and often out of fear that I shall not be believed, seeing how few can believe any but egotistical and sordid motives, I seldom refer to the deepest reason that actuates my conduct.

Consciousness not only makes cowards of us all, but pushes us to be unfair to ourselves. In conduct it is too easy to be more than just to oneself, but not in thought.

6

There is another illusion I have suffered from for the greater part of my earthly existence and have not yet dispelled, though it has thinned and lifted not a little. It is that I am lazy. It has haunted me in all I was doing, and dogged my steps wheresoever I was going. "I ought to be at work," and work meant and still means but one thing: writing for print, composing articles and books. Strenuous days spent in galleries and churches, research, reading—no, that was not work. It took an alarming breakdown, due to what doctors declared was overwork, to make me wonder whether after all I had been so indolent.

The illusion in this instance may be of puritanical origin. Travel, museums, churches, books, photographs, reading, took no effort. They were pleasure. Writing alone came hard, tried one's strength of will to overcome obstacles, put patience to the proof. Writing, not letters to friends but, I repeat, writing for print, was the only activity that I could call work. For that I seldom felt disposed and have not yet overcome the reluctance.

I say again what I have said already, that I was born for conversation and not for writing books. I should have lived in the eighteenth century, when talk was appreciated instead of being, as now, almost despised by the governing classes and looked upon as mere entertainment by the few who can enjoy it. Of course I do not mean when I speak of talk to include oratory, lecturing, preaching. Nor do I include the performer, the verbal soloist, such as among my acquaintances Oscar Wilde, Montesquiou and d'Annunzio were. I have in mind talk which animates the listener and is animated by him, stimulates each to openings of mind, to lightning flashes of suggestion, to entertaining ideas that neither party would have come to by himself—not at the moment, at all events, and perhaps never. And conversation should have the same privilege that is granted—reluctantly enough—to the other fine arts, the privilege of freedom from utilitarian purpose.

The result may be of little consequence, as eighteenth-century conversation doubtless was; the more so as in that least unhappy of centuries a larger number of people were enjoying talk than at any previous moment in history, even if we include the Athens of that greatest of all conversationalists, Plato's Socrates.

To me it has always seemed barbarous, as well as not particularly intelligent, to decry talk, real talk I mean, the stimulating exchange of ideas—not cackle, or chatter, or genealogy, or *couchades*—to despise talk and to exalt action.

How often have I seen quoted, in articles, essays and books, the unhappy phrase of the young, barely emergent Goethe "im Anfang war die Tat." The fully grown-up Goethe may have returned to the opening sentence of the Fourth Gospel. What in effect is "die Tat," the Italian *cosa fatta capo ha?* Who questions that actions have immediate results, that words have not? Let us, however, not stop there, and cheer the result as if it were a bride, greeting it with the *Lohengrin* wedding march. Let us not fail to look at the creature and see what sort of wench she is. Is she going to make us happy or to make us miserable, add to our House of Life or diminish, adorn or befoul it?

It is juvenile, it is thoughtless and reckless, to act, "act in the living present heart within and" —the Irrational overhead. We have been doing so for a century and more, ever since the triumphs of Romanticism, and look where we are this blessed year of grace 1940!

Creative fruitful action is preceded if not generated by talk, talk, talk, endless talk night and day: the eighteenth-century talk, that prepared minds for the French Revolution and made its triumph so easy. Despite all the horrors of the upheaval, horrors inseparable from any and every social one, the permanent results of that revolution are among the most beneficent in history. Even the Soviet Revolution owes much not only to the kind of talk of the intelligentsia for generations past, as we Westerners know it best from Turgeniev and Dostoievsky, but also to the talk during the first World War of the millions of mobilized but unemployed peasants, who for lack of armaments were never called to the front and had nothing to do in their barracks but discuss events and to hear all about the corruption, confusion and incompetence of the government they were serving. Their loyalty as well as their trust were undermined, and when the crash came all were surprised that the peasantry, supposed to worship the Czar as God-on-earth and to love the Church with filial devotion, lifted no finger in their defence or so much as showed signs of regretting them.

To sum up: Men of action appear only when the ground has been prepared for them; and talk has a large share in their preparation. The quality of the talk has no small influence on the results. A "Napoleon" was, so to speak, the coagulation and crystallization of the highly cultivated talk of disinterested spirits in Paris salons, while Hitler and Stalin are the incarnate post-hypnotic suggestions of the resentful, rabid, self-educated haranguing that went on in Bavarian beer cellars and of the neolithic chatter among Russian peasant recruits in their barracks. As for Italy, the Fascist regime has been put together out of two elements, the syndicalists and the imperialists. Of the last, the only one I can speak of with authority, D'Annunzio was the prophet, precursor and Tyrtaeus not only as poet and novelist but as talker, exercising a more direct, more vital, more permeating influence through fresh than through canned speech. And what talk did not go on in favour of the integral restoration of the Empire of the

Caesars among Italian "burjui" classes, in the salons and clubs of the titled, and in the cafés of the untitled!

If talk is as inoperative as the admirers of action claim, why is it that institutions, lay and ecclesiastical, have had to employ their fullest police-power to counter it with the talk not only of their paid agents but of the heads of governments? Nowadays it goes so far that the subjects of authoritarian regimes are on frequent occasions compelled to listen to this countertalk, and at intervals with religious devotion to the rulers themselves.

And, besides, who is the man of action? Is it Attila, Genghis Khan, Tamerlane, Charles XII? Or is it rather a Caesar, a Mohammed, a Napoleon, a Bismarck? The first batch and legions of their kind have trampled everything under them, acting in the living present, leaving nothing but devastation and death to the immediate future. The others have left far more than destructive results although God knows there were enough of these too. But they were great talkers and were or could have been great writers as well. Caesar, according to all accounts, was a brilliant conversationalist and we know that he was a considerable writer. Mohammed, if we may take what is supposed to be his table talk, the *Hadith,* to witness, must also have been a most stirringly eloquent talker, and what a poet he was we see in the finer suras of the *Koran.* Napoleon was a most fascinating talker and a wonderful writer. As for Bismarck, he had much of our Dr. Johnson about him as a talker and could have been a great man of letters if in an evil day he had not taken to politics.

Was Socrates a man of action? Was the Buddha, was Jesus, was Confucius? To whom do we nowadays owe more, to Alexander and Caesar or to Socrates and Jesus? To whom does Asia owe more, to its ferocious, reckless, berserker men of action, mere names to us, or to Confucius and Sakya Muni, although these last, like Socrates and Jesus, only talked and talked? The answer is contained in the phrase of universal currency: "The pen is mightier than the sword." We must add, "And the tongue mightier than the pen." Socrates, Jesus and the Buddha talked and never wrote.

It seems clear that the present war is largely the outcome of too much energizing, too much producing, too much need of placing the product, too much need of far and near conquest in order to place our products. Not only that, but the great powers were like loaded trains running with lightning speed along the same track. Collision and crash were inevitable.

Dare we be optimistic enough to hope that, after fighting has stopped, due reflection will lead us to limit production severely and the activities leading to it? If so, how can we hope to employ our leisure better than in enlightened and humanizing talk?

7

Returning to self, I must speak of still another illusion I have not succeeded in dispelling. It is that I might have made more of it. Not in a worldly way, not by way of power or place, or recognition—none of these and kindred things. What I fear is that I have not borne the fruit that as a plant I should have brought to full ripeness. Of all careers suitable to my make-up, have I pursued the one that got the best out of me? In the career I have followed, have I always chosen the most spiritually profitable fields? I fear not. I cannot rid myself of the insistent inner voice that keeps whispering and at times hissing, "You should not have competed with the learned nor let yourself become that equivocal thing, an 'expert.' You should have developed and clarified your notions about the enjoyment of the work of art. These notions were your own. They were exhalations of your own vital experience. They were no echo or sediment of what you had heard and what you had read. You should have elaborated these notions, using your previously published but undefended statements as themes for exposition and discussion, rather than to leave them the way you did, thrown down as axioms. Having done which, you should have applied these notions now bodied forth as theories, you should have tried to treat the other arts in the same way, not only the visual but the verbal and musical."

The inner voice goes on to say: "Recall the summer of 1895. You had the *Florentine Painters* behind you. You were a wanderer in Germany. You were alone, you had no company but your thoughts. You wanted no other, for these thoughts made you happy with what they revealed, with what they penetrated, with what they irradiated. Your mind worked as never before and, shame, never since. You had visions, clear, detailed visions of what you should do for years and years to come—a lifetime, in fact. Remember, you mapped out one book on ideated sensations, and another on life-enhancement, and a third on the portrait. Instead of accepting this revelation as the light to guide you for the rest of your days, as the Pisgah sight of your promise, you let yourself be seduced into undertaking a work on the Drawings of the Florentine Painters. How could you be so easily lured away from the path that divine guidance had opened and lit up for you?"

Yes, I remember. My brain was teeming with ideas. One was that if we were only gifted enough we should not want to perpetuate a work of art, unless it was necessary for daily life, like the houses we lived in, the buildings we worked in and the gardens and parks we breathed in. If we were as sure of producing each day a painting, a sculpture, a poem, a piece of music as satisfactory to our minds and hearts as our daily food was to our bodies, we should want it, so to speak, fresh from the oven. The day's leisure would be filled with the enjoyment of the day's masterpieces with no time, energy, or desire to look backward to what had been created the day before and all the days before that day. I was fascinated by the idea and was spinning it out and embroidering it till it flashed upon me that we should then be but instinctive animals, exercising gifts superior to those of bird and beaver, singing and weaving and constructing, but as unconscious of past and future. I recalled that it was the ever present sense of the past, of what mankind had already achieved, that distinguished us from the rest of creation. The least advanced of our species have regard for their immediate forebears, and as they get more civilized they acquire more and more interest in what their clan and tribe and people have been before them. Many stop short at their family trees, far branched enough to necessitate much memory, and at the doughty deeds of their ancestors, the warrior classes down to the armigerous of this day. Others try to embrace, and if they cannot embrace long to know, the autobiography of the entire race from the first dawn of consciousness, its many sorrows and compensating joys, its achievements, its constructions, its dreams, its yearnings, its triumphs and defeats as embodied in its stories, its songs, its temples, its palaces, its country seats, its town dwellings, its music, its dancing. In a word the completest human being, as distinct from no matter how superior a mere animal, is the man of culture, and he is that because he has the fullest and most cheering and most inspiring sense of what man has been and therefore still may be.

I could retort to the voice, "All about me, ever since I left Harvard, it was said that I was loafing, that I was wasting my best years in mere amusement, that the little I had published was no proof that I could or did work. I dared not resist the chance offered of proving that I could toil and plod and pedantize and bore with the best of them."

Ten years (if I include both editions) were spent on this task. I cannot say wasted. This book, to my limited knowledge, started the relatively new, if not entirely new, approaches to the study of an artist's drawings, apart from their intrinsic value as creations, to which also more attention was given than ever before perhaps. Moreover, it was the first time that the attempt was made to study what drawings remained out of the entire output of a school of painters. The two chief novelties referred to were, first, the inclusion of the drawings as an integral part of the artist's creativeness, and valued at least as much as his finished work; the other, the light the sketches for a given picture throw on the creative process of the artist as well as upon his individual gifts. Was he, for instance, a born painter like, say, Titian, or a born draughtsman like Michelangelo?

To-day no monograph on an artist is published that does not take into account his drawings as much as his completed works. That it is so may be partly the result of my approach to the subject in *The Drawings of the Florentine Painters.*

The same result might not have followed had I written the few pages in which I could have stated and explained how to study drawings and left it at that. The mind, it has often been remarked, seems as unable to live on extracts only as the body. Both require mere bulk. The difference is that nature has made tolerable provisions for elimination from intestines, and medicine supplies purges. Neither God nor man has yet invented a way of ridding the mind of useless and false knowledge. Hence the famous phrase of Josh Billings: "The trouble with people is not that they don't know but that they know so much that ain't so."

And yet it is a pity that I spent so many years on a task which others might have done as well once the path was laid out. The little satisfaction that accrued from the completion of the work could not quiet a gnawing conviction that I should have spent ten years to better purpose than to prove that one could be a systematic worker.

This book, in two folios too heavy to lift, has never been seriously reviewed either in the first edition or in the second, but with the public estimation it established my reputation as an authority. That reputation alone would have cost me the friendship of some of my close adherents, no small sacrifice. One of them came to me during my annual visit to London and told me with a choking voice that in Bond Street my word was law, and that it stood in the way of his career. To me at the moment it meant nothing, nor could I conceive that this fellow student would turn not into an adversary but an out and out enemy. Perhaps I did not reflect that I, too, might hanker after authority if I had not possessed it. And having had it for three decades at least may be the reason why I do not miss it, now that it has vanished.

It cost even more. My authority soon sank to something less distinguished, less respectable even. I soon discovered that I ranked with fortune-tellers, chiromancists, astrologers and not even with the self-deluded of these, but rather with the deliberate charlatans. At first I was supposed to have invented a trick by which one could infallibly tell the authorship of an Italian picture. A famous writer on the Renaissance, Vernon Lee, thought it was close and even mean of me not to let her share the secret. Finally it degenerated into a widespread belief that if only I could be approached the right way I could order this or that American millionaire to pay thousands upon thousands and hundreds of thousands for any daub that I was bribed by the seller to attribute to a great master. Proposals of this nature, no matter how decorously veiled, became a nuisance and a burden; and in the end I was compelled in self-defence to refuse to see people unless I was sure that they brought no "great masters" with them. Needless to say that every person I would not receive, every owner whose picture I would not ascribe to Raphael or Michelangelo, or Giorgione, Titian or Tintoretto, etc., etc., turned into an enemy.

Perhaps much if not all of this would have been avoided if I had let myself be solicited to write on other subjects than Italian Renaissance painting. Convinced on the one hand that to know all that at a given moment could be discovered in the exploration of this field, to know enough to be sure one was not humbugging, was a whole-time job; and on the other hand, fully aware of how limited was my capacity for concentrated work, I refused to write, let alone to play the expert, on any question outside my own parish, and refrained from publishing anything on contemporary art. The one exception I can recall to mind confirmed the resolution. It was this: in the *New York Nation* early in this century I happened to read a letter from Paris in which the correspondent spoke of Matisse as a *fumiste* whose only object was to *épater les bourgeois*. It was too much. I took up my pen and sent a short note of protest to set the readers of my favourite and revered weekly to rights. The attention aroused by these few lines of print made me aware of the authority I could wield as a critic of modern art. The entire Stein family, Michael, Sally, Leo, Gertrude, who at the time arrogated to themselves the office of High Protectors of newness in painting, began to prod me to leave all I had and to dedicate myself to expounding the merits of the new school. When I would not, they sadly put me down as having made the great refusal. Other artists approached me from every side. Years later, as the first World War was nearing its chequered end, a lady of fashion insisted on taking me to a studio. She would not tell me whose. Nor would it have enlightened me if she had, never having heard the artist's name before. I was treated to a private show of daubs and absurdities which I enjoyed but moderately. The lady who had brought me tried to stir me to utter some words of appreciation. Finally the painter himself spoke up and said, "You made Matisse. Can't you do the same for me?" He could no more realize than the people who came to have their *croûtes* or forgeries baptized as great masters that there was any "damned merit" in the case, a matter of quality to be considered. Happily this aspirant soon deserted painting for apostolic journalism in book form.

I dreaded the personal element in my job, and that was a contributing and perhaps chief reason why I would not write on contemporary art. My standards were based on what survived of the greatest and best in fifty centuries of creative genius. It would not be fair to measure up against it the product of any single day, not even this day. Yet I had no other balances in which to weigh the artist. Besides I could not forget what one successful painter told me. Critics, he said, who spoke ill of him were malignant charlatans, and braying asses when they praised him. His adjectives were perhaps excessive but his substantives not far from the truth. From us critics, the painter cannot ask for the only observations that interest him, helpful technical ones. He despises our amateurishness and studio gossip. He wants nothing but our help in building up his reputation and selling his pictures.

Among the indigent and most unappreciated of the painters whom the Steins took up and treated with almost maternal solicitude was Picasso. Lest I forget it I record now, as it comes back to my memory: meeting this most protean and acrobatic of painters, the most ready to take any jump, to put on any motley or mask, to twist himself into any shape and always with dazzling dexterity—meeting him after he had become the sovereign idol of the public that writes, that "turtle-eats," that buys, he condescended to recall that he had known me at the Steins' and added, "Ah, those Steins, how they did exploit me!"

It would not be fair to deny that being an authority brought material advantages. Not only did it enable me to pay for assistance in any work, for comfort at home and abroad, and for expensive journeys, but it gave me the means to acquire the books and photographs that my study and research required. The only boast I feel like making is that the library I have accumulated item by item during the last fifty years will enable those who come after me to continue my kind of work for generations to come. It will require relatively little outlay to keep it up to date.

All that. Yet I repeat that I took the wrong turn when I swerved from more purely intellectual pursuits to one like the archæological study of art, gaining thereby a troublesome reputation as an "expert." My only excuse is, if the comparison is not blasphemous, that like Saint Paul with his tent-making and Spinoza with his glass-polishing, I too needed a means of livelihood. Mine did not take up more of my time but very much more of my energy. Those men of genius were not hampered in their careers by their trades. Mine took up what creative talent there was in me, with the result that this trade made my reputation and the rest of me scarcely counted. The spiritual loss was great and in consequence I have never regarded myself as other than a failure. This sense of failure, a guilty sense, makes me squirm when I hear myself spoken of as a "successful man" and as having made "a success of my life." I used to protest but gave it up at last, for nobody would believe that my vehement negatives were more than polite modesty or indeed the conceit of an ambition that had not yet been satisfied. So I now put up with being admired as a success just as after years and years of correcting people for doing so, I put up with being addressed as "Dr." or "Professor," titles I have no right to as I have never had a doctor's degree and still less have I ever occupied a university chair.

On the other hand fairness compels me to say that this absorption in archæological study and research was far from a mere slavery imposed by ambition, or even need. I enjoyed it too much. Indeed I venture to doubt whether anybody has passed through life with so much freedom from forced labour as I have. I was blessed from early years with a knack for throwing myself head over heels into the task before me. There was a moment in my twenties when it looked as if I should have to leave Europe and return to teach in some Western college. The prospect was scarcely pleasing but I recall cheering myself with the confidence that I should end by enjoying it.

And so it was with the *Florentine Drawings.* I was carried on the wings of curiosity. The zest for the work made me beat the pavement with pleasure as I walked from Fiesole to and from the Uffizi, and I was almost ecstatic as I pored over the portfolios in the icy-cold printroom pervaded by the keeper's rank and stale cigar smoke.

8

Another reason why I have not made more of myself has been an intemperate lust for reading, which has not diminished but grown with the years. I can get absorbed in any historical work regarding any people, any period, any movement in religion or in thought, any anthropological or ethnological publication, the more detailed the better. I can read any book of travel. Memoirs, correspondence entertain me. Narrative carries me with it no matter whither. Only verse has ceased to be a necessity. It is not only because most contemporary verse is a sealed chamber that I have no desire to penetrate: even the verse that I still enjoy and love as one loves and enjoys *die alte Weise,* the songs of Zion, the poems that enraptured the soul and humanized the heart of Europe, even these I no longer thirst for as I used to. Information, interpretation, reflection are what I am after. Something within my range of interest that I have not yet known, an idea accessible to my intelligence that has not occurred to myself, makes me happy with an almost voluptuous happiness.

So I waste time and energy reading and seldom in connection with my task, but freely, irresponsibly, without a pencil and no thought of taking notes. Now, it is a commonplace that the more one loves to read the less one is likely to write. Born writers read as little as born painters look at paintings—excepting their own and those of their pals.

Travel likewise debauched me. I could follow up any road, any bypath, with the same zest that I would read a story, for the fun of going on and on. I have not yet got over the small boy's dread of a journey coming to an end. Once started, I do not want to stop. On the pretext of having to see certain works of art, and to see them where they grow, I make costly tours and give them time that in deepest conscience I suspect of being unnecessary. For the task in hand, the time could have been better spent in the library, with books and photographs. It is there, and not picnicking around, that scholarship is apt to be most creative and productive.

Perhaps there is a further reason for my failure in the fact that I have wasted too much of myself in attempting to establish my position as a *monsieur*—a less ambivalent term than our word "gentleman" which may refer to birth alone, whereas the French term refers to breeding and standing. Seeing I had no roots in any of the countries I was living in, it was but natural, although neither noble nor even wise, to harbour such an ambition, and to resent any question as to my right to a place in society.

Whence came the intimate sense of that right? From the fact that my childhood was spent in an aristocratic republic and, though under Russian rule, all the more aristocratic for being Jewish. There my family was among the first if not the first, and from earliest awareness I was encouraged to regard myself as its future head. There is truth in Caesar's saying: "Better first in a village than second in Rome." I knew from infancy that I was to be the first in my village, and it bred in me a sense of being anybody's social equal that I have never lost. To this day I avoid people who might regard me as an inferior, not because of their merit but through official and social rank.

Finally there is another reason still why I have not made more of myself. Looking back over the years, I realize, as I could not at the time, that while I had a certain vitality I never had the health necessary for sustained effort. Perhaps that is why I tended to take to occupations that came easy and did not require such efforts. Perhaps too that is why I was so ready to yield to mere curiosity and to disperse interest in so many directions.

9

These reasons may be no more than anyone might give when asked to state what were the adverse circumstances that prevented his manifesting the genius of which undoubtedly he was possessed. Who so humble as not to fancy what he might have been! I cannot forget that when still an undergraduate at Harvard, Charles Eliot Norton said to Barrett Wendell who repeated it, "Berenson has more ambition than ability." Norton never changed his mind. I sent him my virgin work, the *Venetian Painters of the Renaissance.* In his note of acknowledgment he expressed surprise that it should have been left to me to write on that subject. He protested vigorously against my venturing to give naturalization papers, as it were, to Japanese art and ranking Carlo Crivelli for his essential qualities with those lacquers, rather than with European painting. I did not feel encouraged to send him other books of mine. He wrote a long review of my *Lorenzo Lotto,* taking it as a serious but mistaken effort, mistaken in method and mistaken in purpose, for Lotto was not worth the trouble. Years later, when my *Drawings of the Florentine Painters* was put on sale, he discouraged the Harvard Library from purchasing a copy. It was no satisfaction to me that afterwards they did buy it at an enhanced price. So much for the present about Professor Norton. Another occasion may induce me to say more about him, his charm, his good and great influence not only over the young, breezy and not always high-bred barbarians who already were snobbizing Harvard, but over marginals like myself, on the ragged edge of the social body, with nothing to recommend them but their Pandora's box of personal gifts and characteristics.

"Ambition"—but what is ambition in a college junior or senior! Could it be called by anything so serious? I was living in a magical world where everything might be and nothing need be. Of the "real world"—so called by the grownups, the hard-boiled—I knew little or nothing. Not that I had not touched squalor and sordidness, meanness and brutality. They seemed necessary conditions of existence, unavoidable and to be thought about as little as possible. My longings were already for an earthly paradise, a state of adolescent bliss, destined progressively to be in the first place a happy hunting ground—that is to say, a condition where one could exercise one's functions in most satisfying fashion—then for a New Jerusalem; and finally for a City of Man where one would use nature as a quarry to build up a life as far beyond mere nature as a splendid edifice is beyond the stone in the hillside. In my last term or two at Harvard I was looking forward to the years after graduation as to a time in which I could begin to realize what there was in me. No doubt I was as ignorant of myself as of the world I was to encounter, both plunged as yet in magic and mirage. No doubt I cherished fantastic hopes, harboured absurd wishes, conceited expectations. Yet I had not exactly a sobering sense of reality—but a warning scepticism. It chimed in with what William James happened to say at that time in the lecture-room: that we youngsters might have hopes as extravagant as we could frame, but that meanwhile we were happy with any payment on account, no matter how modest. I will not—not just now, at all events—detail what I expected would happen when I started active life. I recall distinctly that I did not hanker for place or power, nor for the palm without the strife. I wanted to exercise my functions and already had the inner security that doing so would lead me to what I wanted out of life. *"War es so niedrig was ich da dachte!"* That was the only ambition to possess me, but it did master me. And after all, despite the genuine sense of failure inspired by the pattern I had for my career, I have got out of life what I most deeply desired, even if I have achieved little.

Goethe thought that what youth truly craved for old age yields in abundance. Perhaps. Only one must distinguish widely between wishing and willing, and reflect that the will effectively disposes while the wish merely proposes. In the case of the private person, as in the conduct of the body politic, it is seldom that the end worked for is the product of the means employed. Needless to add, the word "will" is used here not in the sense of a determination to do or acquire or attain, but of the unchanging, unswerving tendencies of personality and its momentum, if you like. Perhaps it is what the Freudians mean by the *libido,* only that this term reeks of the pan-erotic, the doctrine that the individual, the human individual, is governed for the most part from below the belt. No doubt the reproductive organs have an importance that some nature-despising and world-denying systems of thought—not all, least of all many Church Fathers and Doctors—have attempted to ignore. That offers no excuse for plunging into an opposite excess, and affirming that we are mere carriers of our genitals and that the mind exists only to serve them and further their itches and tumefactions. The Greek herma, it will be remembered, recognizing that a healthy male was aware only of head and genitals in his body, represented these only, leaving the rest as a pillar, but subordinating the animal to the spiritual.

10

I have wondered ever since psycho-analysis has been the fashion whether after a certain age, say somewhere between fifty and sixty, more people were not concerned with constipation rather than with sex. It can get to be at least as much of a preoccupation, an obsession; and intestinal relief as eagerly awaited as ever sex relief in earlier years.

There is a famous anecdote that takes on a different aspect and lends itself to a less cynical explanation than is usually given it. Prince Gorchakov had been Russian chancellor for decades. He was over eighty, and at long last the time had come to retire. One morning he called together his entire staff to say good-bye and greeted them with the words: "Friends, you will be glad to hear that I have had a satisfactory evacuation this morning." He thought it was the best account he could give of his health to people whom he expected to take an interest.

Did not the Elders of Israel (not in their *Protocols* but in the Talmud somewhere) pronounce the proper functioning of the intestine as so much of Paradise? "Paradise" was obviously their equivalent for the French word *volupté* which means more than our word "pleasure" yet nothing like so much as our "voluptuousness." La Fontaine in his *Invocation* could not conceivably have addressed himself to *volupté* if to him it meant "voluptuousness" or even "pleasure."

While on this subject, so frankly entertained by Mediterranean people to this day with enviable naturalness, I am reminded of a bit of folklore told by the rabbi who was teaching me Hebrew when I was a little boy of six at most. We were reading the book of Genesis and in commenting on Pharaoh the teacher told me why the monarch suddenly took to hating Moses who hitherto had been a great favourite. The Pharaoh who had given out that, being a god, he never felt the calls of nature, was one fine morning discovered by Moses satisfying them on the banks of the Nile. Whether this comes from the written lore of the Elders of Israel or was handed down by word of mouth from generation to generation I cannot tell, as I have small acquaintance with the sources. An answer to the same question would be desirable regarding another comment of the same tutor. We were reading about the covenant made between the Lord and Abraham. The rabbi explained that Jehovah and his votary grasped each other's virile members as they took the oath, and I seem to recollect, but am not quite sure, that they swore by the same members.

What Babylonian or Assyrian bas-reliefs reaching back to the first Sargon at least, this calls up! Where did the rabbi get this from, for he surely did not invent it? Perhaps from Genesis 32 : 24, 25. If handed down orally, something equally primitive could as faithfully have been transmitted across the millennia.

Before I have done with this teacher of little boys of six or seven, I shall put down a remark of his that made an indelible impression. It was that, God being infinite, any epithet, any adjective, any predicate applied to Him was blasphemous, because it was necessarily a limitation of His infinitude.

I owe to the reading of the Hexateuch, the historical books and the major Prophets of the Old Testament before I was ten, and to learning much of them almost by heart, two dominant tendencies of my mind. One is an insatiable curiosity about origins in particular, and about history in general. This has been such a source of vivifying and transporting interest that I cannot regret it, although as already confessed, it has led to the self-indulgent dispersal of my energies. The other has proved less comfortable and less valuable. It is the readiness to indignation which finds expression in the Israelitish as well as in the Jewish books of the Old and New Testaments. True, it was for the most part an indignation not against mere oppression or misfortune such as we find early in Egypt and Mesopotamia, in Greece with Homer who shivers at the thought of being the slave of a poor man, or Hesiod with his bitterness over the lot of the small farmer, but indignation against injustice, against what should not be either admitted, or tolerated. A most noble and beautiful advance in humanity but unhappily seldom free from a despairing sense of helplessness and impotent resentment. It fosters states of mind that lead either to the "Ivory Tower," a house full of books and a garden of flowers, or to unreasoned explosions of violence.

Returning for a moment to the interest implanted by the Old Testament, let me add that an early instinct—for it was not inspired or fed by others—urged me to inquire what outside sources had to say about peoples and events there treated; and this urge has all through life returned again and again with ever increased energy. At the minute I am writing, my study is cluttered up with scores upon scores of books in all the languages to me accessible, on Hittites, Hurrites, Amorites, Philistines, Moabites; and I deplore that I can gather no information regarding Peruzites, Jebusites and Hivites. Were the last conceivably the Acheans who in the Tel Amarna texts are supposed to appear as Achivi?

And while on these peoples, dead and gone so long ago, why has no one (to my knowledge) made a study of the struggle between Israelites and Philistines as a typical instance of what went on along all Mediterranean shores between the hinterlanders and the invaders from the sea, whether Aegeans, Phoenicians or Greeks? The Hebrews alone have left record of the ensuing conflicts and of the attitude of the invaded toward the invaders. How little in this case they affected each other! Scarcely a trace of Philistine or Hebrew influence of the one on the other.

11

To return to what I mean by "will": it is not *libido* but what Nietzsche meant by *der Wille zur Macht,* what William James meant when he invented the phrase "the will to believe," Alois

Riegel with his *Kunstwollen*—the will to art, the imperative in taste, the style which imposes itself on society at a given moment, and from which nobody ventures or even wishes to depart.

I have mentioned William James more than once and lest there should be no occasion to speak of him further on, I must put down in writing an anecdote of his lecture-room that returns to my mind. He was sitting lightly, almost swinging on the corner of his desk, holding forth in his zestful, engaging, amusing way. Suddenly a sarcastic puritan popped up from his bench and cried out: "Mr. James, to be serious for a moment," and wanted to protest. Roars of laughter, in which the Professor joined, greeted the impertinence.

Two or three years after Norton made his remark on the disproportion between my ambition and my ability, I was sitting one morning toward the end of May at a rickety table outside a café in the lower town of Bergamo. The matutinal freshness of that spring, almost summer, day was suited to encourage a young man to look upon the near future with appetizing expectation. Opposite me sat a chum I had picked up the year before, soon after I first arrived in Florence. He was half Genoese and half Peruvian, with a slim long face, nose thin and slightly aquiline, delicate sensitive mouth and fine black eyes, black hair too, and of course a dark complexion. His name was Enrico Costa and were I writing memoirs I should have a great deal to say about him. For the moment it must suffice that he was one of the most gifted of men. There was no realm of art and literature into which he could not penetrate and, with instinctive accuracy, make a dash for the best.

Very well. Here was this gifted young man with his intellect, his love of the highest and deepest, and I, who, I must confess, had at twenty vague but radiant hopes of becoming a poet, a novelist, a thinker, a critic—a new Goethe, in short. Here we were sitting at a little table partaking of our morning meal and enjoying it although the coffee was poor and thin, the bread sour and badly baked, the butter sourer. I recall saying, "You see, Enrico; nobody before us has dedicated his entire activity, his entire life, to connoisseurship. Others have taken to it as a relief from politics, as in the case of Morelli and Minghetti, others still because they were museum officials, still others because they were teaching art history. We are the first to have no idea before us, no ambition, no expectation, no thought of reward. We shall give ourselves up to learning, to distinguish between the authentic works of an Italian painter of the fifteenth or sixteenth century, and those commonly ascribed to him. Here at Bergamo, and in all the fragrant and romantic valleys that branch out northward, we must not stop till we are sure that every Lotto is a Lotto, every Cariani a Cariani, every Previtali a Previtali, every Santa Croce a Santa Croce; and that we know to whom of the several Santa Croces a picture is to be attributed," etc., etc.

To this in the swift course of two or three years had vaulting ambitions or, at least, dazzling hopes shrunk. No payment on account this time, but its entire reduction to a relative trifle. Luckily one's daimon, one's will to grow, to achieve, to serve, knew better, and before long I was writing the *Venetian Painters,* my *Lorenzo Lotto* and, earlier than either, an essay on the *Rudiments of Connoisseurship.* By the time I was engaged on the *Florentine Painters,* the ambition to distinguish between a twentieth-rate artist and his closest followers seemed dead. It was brought to life again while working on the *Drawings of the Florentines,* for which reason, among others, as I have already told, I have regarded the undertaking of this task as a wrong turn in my career—and not only wrong but sinful.

The adolescent mind that, expanding like a gas, occupies vast stellar spaces but when coagulated shrinks and contracts to a small globe, is not necessarily a matter of age, although much more easily found in youth. It is a state of palpitating expectation based on inexperience. Eloquent idealists, with few exceptions, and reformers, partake of this mental condition. Like the youth who, when faced by concrete facts, readily submits to commanding the few easiest to handle, the reformers I have known, when confronted by the difficulties of improving an abuse, get alarmed enough to turn into more vehement defenders of things as they are than those they had hitherto attacked. I recall such instances among the intellectuals concerned with that adolescent mirage, the late "League of Nations."

12

To go back to the various reasons that led to my failing to make the most of myself, one of the more serious, as it now seems to me, is that I would not learn to address myself to a public whether in writing or speaking. Possibly I could not have learned to speak or even to lecture. Both require verbal memory and a clear strong voice. I have never been able to memorize with accuracy and my voice, rather husky, soon gives out. But surely I could have learned to write? I do not refer only to the choice of words, to the images, to rhythm, to knowing where to apply the purple patch, where to soft-pedal, and where to resort to the *vox humana*. I might even have adapted myself to the more coloured vocabulary that has become current in recent years and the heightened key in which expository prose is now being written. Where I fall down utterly is in not knowing how to arrange and develop what I wanted to communicate. I have failed to discipline myself, to marshal my arguments in the most effective, the most persuasive and most memorable way. I have not learned to develop a theme, to give it the accompaniment best calculated to attract and hold the reader. I have not been will ing to give the time to learn this trade. The result is that the few, the very few, ideas I have launched have but seldom reached the cultivated person, and then distorted by my failure to present them adequately. As for the more professional reader, the ideas so badly, so nakedly put before him tempted him to deck them out with his own more coloured, better draped garments. Not that he was guilty of plagiarism. Far from it. He grasped the idea so instantaneously that he as instantaneously forgot it had not always been his.

As a matter of fact, my writing, even when addressing myself to a friend in a letter, is rarely, if ever, done with reference to the reader but to a sort of other self with whom I am carrying on a continuous discussion. My natural way of thinking is by way of a dialogue and as a little boy of four or five I used to ask others of my own age whether they could talk to themselves. I was amused to discover that they did not understand my question and concluded that it was no use trying to converse with such dull creatures. Have I perhaps retained too much a sense of being other and therefore not called upon to make myself understood?

From the moment I came to believe that I was not going to be a writer, "style" as such did not seem worth the bother. Why waste time on what was bound to perish soon except in footnotes to learned books. Nor was this dictated by mere indolence. Behind it was an exaggerated, and, as I now believe, misleading worship of the permanent, of awe before the everlasting, the "eternal."

This feeling, that one must strive for the enduring, this promotion of the permanent, the surviving, the eternal, to aesthetic and even moral value has tended to inhibit and even to disperse my energies. I was not going to join the hosts busy in preparing each day the verbal hot rolls forgotten the instant they were gobbled up. Unless I could acquire the illusion that I had something to offer that would be lasting, it seemed only decent to do nothing. The error lay in two facts. First, that one is not the best judge of one's own qualities or usefulness and may under-estimate as easily as over-estimate. The other is that by writing nothing except what one expects to be of the highest order, one risks getting out of practice in writing at all, and getting sterilized in thought as well. Thought needs a stimulus. For me the most effective stimulus comes from talk, preferably with the adolescent-minded. But this flow is accidental, and suffers from the drawback of depending on others. Writing, on the contrary, has the advantage of drawing its inspiration from the blank paper, as well as getting many a hint from the planchette element in the pen, which often knows more and better than the person who wields it.

13

I spoke just now of being haunted by the idea of the enduring, the permanent, the ever contemporary, and let me add the universal. That state of mind tends to make one "far-sighted" in the optician's sense and readier to see, in their proper proportions and right relations, distant objects rather than near ones. Yet there is compensation for that as for most evils. It enables one to recover quickly from momentary despair and rage caused by untoward events, and the revoltingly insolent triumph of evil, and at the same time to look into a future depending on what is most unchanging in human nature and on the earth's surface and climate. For instance, whatever the Nazis may do to-day, the vast Danube basin forms a whole with Vienna as its centre, because it is its market town, its shopping town, its university town, its now multi-secular focus of attraction and meaning to the populations to the east and south of it, as well as to Europe as a whole. Berlin is a more artificial affair; for its reign relies on a less stable equilibrium. A slight shifting of the seasons, not to speak of a slight lowering of the surface, might make it almost uninhabitable; and even before such catastrophes set in, commercial and financial trends might cease to favour it and, under political contingencies, even work against it. The vast population which it dominates is held together too much by the artifices, makeshifts and absurdities of mere politics to assure stability. Out of the dust it rose and to the dust it may as soon return.

Then take the Mediterranean in general and Italy in particular. With Europe turning more and more to the open oceans and Europe itself a mere proboscis on the face of Asia, the midland sea cannot expect to regain the central position it had for the five or six thousand years prior to Magellan's rounding the Cape of Good Hope. The Mediterranean can serve only as a passageway from open ocean to open ocean, and it will be everybody's concern to provide that this passage remains free and unimpeded. It is opposed to everybody else's interest that any one Mediterranean government, still less all united, should have the command of its waters and interfere with its function as a free thoroughfare. Despite every effort to the contrary, thoroughfare it will remain as long as the climatic conditions continue to be what they are. Should another ice age return, the Sahara bloom like the rose, and Europe's population once more be forced to huddle round the Mediterranean, then and only then will the central power of that vast basin regain its ancient importance and dominion.

Speaking of climate reminds me of a presentiment I have about the United States of America: namely, that in the long run it may prove unfit for the white man's habitation, as it may have been to that of previous races. The fact that the mountains stretch from north to south opens the land to the extremes of heat coming from the terrestrial steam-bath, the Caribbean, and the icy blasts from the Arctic Ocean, with no transverse ranges as in Central Europe to interpose between the extremes and to mitigate them. The changes are sudden and violent. I can recall the thermometer rising or falling as much as 60° Fahrenheit in the course of a waking day. Plunge a glass first into hot water and then immediately into cold and it will crack. Surely our veins and arteries are more sensitive than any glass and if they do not crack they wear and tear. All who can leave their work, who can afford to get away, have to spend the winter months in Florida or California, the summer ones on the mountains or by the sea. Our towns are scarcely bearable in those seasons. The rapid and extreme changes tend to make us nervous, overactive, restless, overtired, and to use us up early. Some of our oldest settlers are now represented by offspring too frequently consumptive, queer, or otherwise in decline—if not quite degenerate. Thus it is on the cards that the White Man's experiment of occupying America north of the Rio Grande may turn out a failure, as was the effort of the Red Man before him. When Europeans began to colonize the present United States the Indians in occupation were few. Some calculate, they were a few hundred thousand only for that vast territory, and it has even been suggested that they must have been reduced to that by the Black Death which reached them, doing more havoc among them than it had in Europe. It is more likely that the climatic conditions were the cause and the sufficient reason.

Of course the Redskin, with his little more than mesolithic civilization, could not defend himself as we nowadays can. That may lay the catastrophe for centuries, but not avert it.

14

I am sometimes surprised and at times shocked that we cherish such a sense of security, such an arrogant feeling of mastery on this midget of a planet. A slight caper on its part and no trace of us would remain, and nobody to look for a trace.

I could envy people who regard events, whatever

their natures, as so much weather or as the meaningless turning of Fortune's wheel. Mediterranean people still tend to take that view. Mussolini, receiving a French publicist, gave him a consoling lecture on the course of history: "For a hundred years your Revolution ruled Europe. For another century it is our turn. After that you will be again at the wheel."

One of the Italians who tried to run the Tripolitan show—show in the literal as well as figurative sense—comforted an Arab notable by telling him there was no need for taking things so hard. They, the Arabs, had ruled Sicily for two centuries and now Italians would rule Arabs for as long. Well, what of it! Eat, drink and be merry, for in the long run that only matters, or words to that effect.

But how to get rid of the Judæo-puritanical scheme of history as a tending toward a transcendent consummation which each individual by his conduct can modify, speed or retard? How overcome the teaching which so victoriously permeated me during boyhood and youth in Boston and Harvard: the teaching that good was the norm and evil the unusual? That men and women with few exceptions were acting with goodwill from the best motives. I was so addicted to these doctrines, and so keenly aware that I was not living up to their teaching, that I expected everybody to be better and behave better than I did. While I admitted that single individuals might be naughty or worse, so that even now I discover with a certain relief, that so-and-so whom I had revered for his moral superiority is not better than myself, it never occurred to me during my earlier years to think that the rulers of our countries, that the intentions of our governments, could be inspired by any but the highest principles, far beyond those expected of the individual.

Great was my indignation to discover that the contrary prevailed, that nations as corporate entities were not expected to act humanely and scarcely to pretend to any morality whatever; that on the contrary such an entity need consult no law human or divine for its conduct, that it could be as cannibal as it pleased without encountering sincere moral reprobation, except from those it robbed, ravished, and massacred.

It has been a corroding source of bitterness from which I suffer so keenly that too often it drives me to express myself in ungentle speech and even in unparliamentary language.

How much better if, without making children and young people hard-hearted, we could teach them to expect a minimum from us poor bipeds, mere earth bubbles, humanized fully in perhaps no single instance, and as masses scarcely ever. What right have we to expect more from creatures who but a few thousand years ago were no better than the beasts of the field, nay worse, for these seldom kill their own kind for food whereas man did universally and, here and there in the less mechanized societies of the world, still does. So near are we even now to killing for food that few people on the European continent disapprove in their hearts of one country falling upon the other, murdering a suitable number of inhabitants, possessing themselves of their goods, and enslaving the rest. What is the doctrine of *Lebensraum,* the German word for what *we* used to call "the need of expansion" or "manifest destiny," if not communal cannibalism?

So one should avoid expecting the best possible, or even the good, but rest contented with the least bad, the lesser evil. That surely would be a wiser approach not only to national but even to private relations. In other words if you want to be taken for an optimist, cheering the event that can be defended as the smaller evil, you must be a pessimist, that is to say one who expects little from human nature, still so overwhelmingly animal, still so remote from the humanization to which some of us are trying to submit it, with so little apparent success.

15

As early as my college days I was determined not to play the clown or court fool to their Highmightinesses the Public, that public for which, as a child of the aristocratic and cultured ghetto, I had been taught to have nothing but contempt. Again, a grave error. By playing the jester to the same public what an influence, what authority for good—and alas, for evil as well!—has not been exercised by a Bernard Shaw, a Chesterton, or even a Belloc, not to speak of our Dooley.

Poor Oscar Wilde would have been happy with the authority and worship that rewarded a Bernard Shaw, who is favoured with a freedom from inhibitions which has enabled him to become, not the *jongleur* of the Blessed Virgin of the tender mediæval tale, but court fool, clown-in-chief to the Anglo-Saxon middle classes of the mind. Perhaps if the offended and enraged masses just referred to, headed and led by that Philistarch Carson, had not hounded Wilde to a revolting end, there would have been less demand for the rather obvious wit and paradoxes of his more Bohemian fellow Irishman.

Poor Oscar! Well do I remember how in the early nineties he used to tumble into my rooms in North Street, Westminster, exhausted with the effort of entertaining the barbarians and disappointed with the result. "But why do you do it?" "They fascinate me. They are more alive, they breathe a finer air, they are so much more free than we are."

Although fully ten years his junior I used to point out to him that what they showed him was their dress parade, that their barrack life, so to speak, their drill sergeants, were probably as hard as and perhaps more bitter than ours. Much better to play the court fool to these barbarians than to desire or to expect to be accepted as one of them.

16

I have been rambling on over the drawbacks and disadvantages of being too much influenced and directed by the permanent, the enduring, and their kindred value, the universal. Clearly I have been too much under their sway. On the other hand I owe them an easy detachment from the fads, crazes and fanaticisms of the moment, not in the realm alone where the sheltered and safe citizen can enjoy the poets and story-writers who present him pictures of life, the exact opposite of his own, but so remote, so unlikely to touch him that they give him by reaction delicious shivers of escape from danger. I owe them the "other-mindedness" which makes it almost impossible to adhere wholeheartedly to any exclusive scheme of things, to any one church, to any one part, to respond to any "slogan"—revolting word—to be wholly taken in by any appeal to sentiment or to submit to any assault on the heart.

I can recall but one instance of my being completely taken in politically. It was after the last war, the war of 1914-1918 that was going to end wars. I remember my amazement, walking one day during the armistice in the spring of 1919, to see fresh barracks going up in the eastern suburbs of Hyères. I was convinced that they were useless. So it has turned out as we now see—in February 1941—but not in the sense in which I then believed.

A strong feeling for the universal! In nations as well as in individuals inhabiting different countries I see ever so much more similarity than dissimilarity. The individual I meet in England, France, Germany or Italy is, in all but language and what language carries with it, pretty much the same human being. In reading their poets, story-tellers, philosophers and teachers, or a foreign interpreter like Pearl Buck, even the Chinaman is much like the rest of us. I could not revel, as I do, in Leskov's accounts of humble as well as landed and town folk in Russia if their reactions were very different from my own. Indeed, what do we mean by a great writer if not one that not only his own countrymen but all mankind can understand? National differences are in fact so superficial that on acquaintance they disappear. First impressions are therefore the most vivid, and that is why it is difficult to write about a country or an individual one knows well, for the differences evaporate altogether or get too subtilized.

So too in the huge cloudy spaces of art, art in the widest sense, art including all efforts at expression and communication by sound or sight that are not merely utilitarian, I fancy I see through the new phraseology, the new rhythm, and soon guess whether behind them there is anything of universal and permanent value, or merely the popular tune of the day.

While what I have just said about individuals being so much alike despite differences of language, country and habits is still fresh in our minds, let me recount what happened one evening on a visit I was making some thirty-five years ago to Boston. I was invited to dine at Rhodes, the historian's, to meet a score or so of prominent as well as cultured citizens. Knowing that since I had left them I had spent most of the years in Italy, they politely tried to draw me out and asked among other questions what Italians looked like. I glanced around at these Boston worthies, all of uncontaminated Anglo-Saxon blood, and said: "Gentlemen, everyone of you could pass for an Italian, and as far as appearances goes there is not one of you who could not be a Milanese, a Piedmontese, a Venetian, a Florentine, or member of a distinguished family from Rome, Naples or Palermo."

The truth is that it is only the less evolved man or woman who has stamped indelibly on his mask the map of his country. The stage Englishmen or Frenchmen are caricatures.

17

Let me return to the attempt I am making to explain to others, to possible readers, what sort of a person I am. I was saying that, among the reasons that led to my being in my own eyes anything but a successful man, failure to acquire the technique of composition must rank as a principal one. In truth I possess no technique of any sort except the one that has led to the kind of success that I regard as a merely worldly one, not at all the one my soul aspired to. That aspiration was for getting out of myself what would have given me happiness while it procured me the satisfaction of serving others as guide in their gropings, as moulder of thoughts they could not shape, as the magician who could utter the revealing, transmuting, inspiring word. So much depends on technique! Genius has it in the cradle but with pitiless industry others can acquire it to some degree.

I shall not go on enumerating all the causes of failure that I can think of. Besides, the more I thought the more would they increase. There is, however, one more I must refer to. It is that I have lacked the gift of inspiring confidence and loyalty, two qualities of which I myself had a great provision at the start. Experience scarcely diminished confidence in confidence, although I was constantly falling a victim to it, as a constitutional fault or bad habit. The suspiciousness it gave place to was never strong enough to be effective. But loyalty (to my recollection) I have never betrayed. It was the more distressing to discover faithlessness and even treachery in quarters where least expected. If it was the sort that derives from professional jealousy, envy and spite with which, as already hinted, I had encounters enough in my successful years, I should not have been so confounded—a strong word but scarcely too strong. It antedated my career, and in early manhood, as I was leaving college, it began to dawn on me that some people did not take to me, that others disliked me, and that many spoke ungently of me. I on the contrary was as well disposed to others, so ready to meet them more than half way, so little out for anything except to please and to be pleased on a disinterested, almost aesthetic plane, that it not only chilled me and made me unhappy to have my glow of friendly feelings encountered and repelled by icy currents of indifference or even dislike, but it left me amazed and puzzled.

I have not entirely solved the puzzle nor got out of the maze. Yet in time it began to dawn upon me that perhaps I was exorbitant in supposing, although innocently enough, that others would accept the intrusion of my egoism, my claims upon their attention, my eagerness to be heard and to be appreciated and accepted. Perhaps they could not brook my naive presumption that they would welcome what may have seemed to them pretensions to superiority, what to them may have smelt of arrogance if not impudence. In short, and to use my own jargon, they may have felt my company to be more life-diminishing than life-enhancing.

A certain trait of character to which I came rather early in life, or at least became aware of while still a mere lad, must have offered a handle for dislike. It was the precipitous retreat from discussion the moment I realized it was leading nowhere; whether because the people engaged could not believe that they were unfit to carry it on, or that they wanted to have the last word of an argument. Disputation was not to my taste. Except in the field of pure science, and perhaps not even there, disputation and argument seldom attempt to elucidate or to persuade tactfully. They prefer to overwhelm brutally. Frederick the Great is credited with saying, "I take the territories I want and leave it to my jurists to justify me!" I confess I find pretty much the same prevailing in scholarship as distinct from pure science. The endless footnotes flooding the few lines of text in archæological and historical works, not to speak of such malodorous swamps as anthropology, sociology, politics and kindred writing, are, in themselves, so neutral that they serve equally to affirm what the last generation has denied as what the next will affirm again. But to return to the microscopic homunculus, myself, I am sure I gave offence in acting as if I did not think people were worth talking to, whereas it was only that I wanted to change the subject, *umsteigen,* in Mark Twain's phrase, to topics less controversial, more amiable, more amusing. But no, some folk will insist on behaving like a monkey on a stick, and never stop till they have exhibited to their abundant satisfaction those traits in themselves which others are perchance least eager to see.

Genius is so universally life-enhancing that the only way to withstand it is to exclude it altogether in the way stiff society did till not so long ago, the way the gentlefolk made their host remove Werther from an assembly as recounted in the youthful Goethe's never ageing tale. Genius rises above envy and spite, but one with no claims to that is apt to be more disliked and combated for his good qualities than for his bad ones, for what stands in the way of others rather than for what these are confident is inferior and weaker than in themselves.

I soon made a discovery that in some ways was still worse. I had flatteringly assumed that I was unique in my way and could not be replaced. Let me add that I attributed the same qualities to all individuals and to a great degree I still do so. At all events I avoid frequently those who do not impress me that way. What was my dismay to learn that what people liked in me they could with seeming ease find elsewhere. Still greater was my unhappiness to recognize that even in love one could so easily be replaced—more easily, perhaps. For much in the love between the sexes is physical or chemical and little is left for individuality. Fundamentally sex is indifferent to its object. As a French saying has it: All wines are good enough. So with sex. Cynics know this and hence are called "cynics," but youth, for all its romanticism, practices it assiduously, as do the romantics of all ages. What wine-taster, what man athirst, thinks of the bottle which is to give him drink? "Why bother about the decanter if the wine is good!" The quality of the flagon as an artifact or work of art will be appreciated only by the connoisseur who enjoys it for itself and never asks what it was meant to contain.

18

More recently, I mean in the last twenty years or so, I began to discover that I intimidated, that I frightened, people. Only the other day the husband of an old friend confessed that he had always been afraid of me. I looked at him with startled eyes. He went on to say that my mind worked much more clearly, quickly and deeply than his. Flattering, no doubt, but if I have not ceased enjoying admiration I have long since preferred affection. For this I crave more and more. The other neither warms nor cheers me. So my old friend's explanation augmented the unhappiness I have long been feeling over the fact that I frighten people. I am not referring to the shyness touched with awe, inspired by the reputation for having mastered one's trade and being an authority on a subject, nor to the vague but somewhat chilling respect instinctively felt towards the old who still enjoy the free use of head, belly and members. No. I fear it is something in my conversation. I fear I still have a way of rebutting what others have to say before they can enjoy the satisfaction of coming out with all that they want to say, thereby leaving them with a feeling of resentful frustration, of not having been allowed to perform their stunt. And I am or have been too intolerant of relatively innocent humbugs, relatively harmless pretentiousness. In a sense it is bad luck that, not temperamentally disposed to suffer fools gladly, I yet, owing to my reputed place in the fields of art and letters, attract the "culture-snobs" as I call the people who hover around those of us who may supply them with appetizing tidbits for the tea fight, the luncheon hour or the dinner table. Impatience used to get the better of me as it may again on provocation, and a freezing remark would send them off scarcely to sing my praise.

A chilly if not an out-and-out hostile atmosphere toward one can be created and spread by the people who have disliked one on aesthetic or social grounds only, spread to others who are sufficiently attentive to the sound of a name known just enough to attract curiosity but too little informed to be proof against what they hear. They start all sorts of gossip, tending to make one deserve their ill will. Thus it has happened to me again and again that I have received ladies courteously and learned shortly afterwards they had heard me say this or that that I had not said but was in character with the myth that I was becoming. For a person who has made any sort of name for himself cannot avoid becoming a myth. If he is in public life, his party will make him into one in accordance with the use that they have for him. If he is a writer or artist or a star of the opera, stage, or film, the myth is shaped quickly by the publisher, the reviewer, the art dealer with his train of bleating or venal critics, by the impresario with his advertising agencies of propaganda. Even the college professor becomes a myth to the freshers and sophs who have not yet come under his influence; and professors survive in memory as myths rather than as persons—in the golden recollection of far-away college days.

The various categories just enumerated enjoy a certain protection from their very popularity, from being so much exposed to the public gaze. But one like myself, belonging to no group, to no society claiming him as its own and sheltering and defending him almost automatically, one who, on the contrary, through heredity and circumstances if not by temperament, would be a stranger everywhere, and singularly so living in a country far from the land, the men, the women, the customs, the ideas, the ideals, the commonplaces, the catchwords, the gossip, the old and new memories where he grew to youth and matured to manhood—one like myself was particularly marked out for being converted into a myth shaped by every kind of prejudice, favourable and unfavourable, the latter chiefly, owing to the proneness of human nature to lap up and retain evil communications rather than charitable ones. I was the more exposed as with the years and growing reputation I retired more and more into a shell embracing geographically all the earth, yet far from the drawing-rooms, Bloomsburys, Greenwich Villages of London, New York, Paris and "way-stations." I have seldom put in an appearance in those high places since the beginning of the epoch-making new era: the outbreak, in 1914, of the still continuing war.

Let me recount an anecdote in this connection. Many years ago at the Florence station my wife and I got into a railway compartment to go to Venice. Just before starting a young woman bustled in and, as she did not look unpleasant and was obviously New England, I made room for her and helped with her bags. We started and settled down to reading. I cannot recall whether it was she or I that opened a volume of Santayana's masterpiece, *The Life of Reason,* fit to be placed beside the books of wisdom composed by Greek Stoics and Alexandrian and Palestinian Jews in the century or two before and after the earthly life of Christ. Nor can I remember which of us two was indiscreet enough to spy out what the other was perusing. Probably it was I, devoured as I always am with curiosity to know what anybody in my presence is reading. At all events she began to express her admiration of Santayana and his work. I joined in whole-heartedly and between us we recited an antiphony in his praise. Suddenly her voice changed. Harshly and huskily she broke out with: "But there is another Harvard man, a contemporary of Santayana's, now being read, and him I just can't bear. I detest him.

His name is Be—" I did not let her finish. I said: "Berenson, yes, that is myself."

What is odd is that the moment she changed key and began to talk disparagingly, I suspected, indeed I knew, it was I she had in mind. How did I know it? How is it that I often get the full quality of a work of art at the instant of infinitesimal duration between my seeing it and becoming aware of looking at it?

But I cannot refrain from telling another anecdote in connection with Santayana and his more systematized and up-to-date Hellenic, Hebraic and Emersonian wisdom.

I was holding forth about him at a small luncheon party given by a distinguished civil servant in St. James's Place and the fascinating lady on my left took fire and flamed up with eagerness to try him for herself. As she belonged to a family that read books over and above the railway guide, Whitaker's Almanac, society memoirs and the current novel, I hastened to Mr. Bain to address to her the entire *Life of Reason*. I was thanked charmingly and was assured that it would be read incessantly from cover to cover, volume by volume. Time passed and Logan Pearsall Smith brought out a selection of tidbits from this work. The lady, as Bain told me afterwards, was among the first to acquire a copy.

19

Then there are the people who take a dislike to one and betray an antipathy for no reason whatever:

"I do not like you, Doctor Fell. You ask me why—
I cannot tell." I have at times wondered what my instinctive and instantaneous reaction would be if I could meet myself for the first time. This has all but happened. More than once it has occurred that somewhat absent-mindedly I was mounting a broad staircase which at the landing had a pier-glass rising from floor to ceiling. I seemed to see coming toward me a figure not particularly to my taste, not at all corresponding to the type I naturally liked; and this figure had an abstracted effaced expression that I should rather sidle away from than be drawn to. All this before recognizing that it was myself.

Many would change for better looks, for a more serviceable body, for a less disagreeable character and for a sweeter temper. Marcus Aurelius is not alone in believing that we are little souls carrying corpses. A great lady with whom I had a tangential acquaintance was found gloomily rocking in a chair. "What is the matter?" asked an intimate. "How would you feel," she answered, "if like me you had to pass the rest of your days between a big bosom and a bigger behind?" Saint Bernard himself could hardly surpass that, even though he did use more "realistic" language.

20

Impatience, perhaps my dearest sin, has not only made me enemies. It has discouraged me from taking part in any kind of public life. I do not refer to impatience with benevolence or malevolence due to foolishness, ignorance, pettiness or greed but to an aversion for employing hours or even minutes in a way and to a purpose not my own. Early in life, long before I was aware of it, I had elevated time into the ultimate if not the sole currency and was ready to buy it with anything I could dispose of. To waste it drives me frantic.

I recall going to Paris in 1917 when we entered the war, eager to do my bit. An influential friend recommended me to the head of a department lodged in splendour on the first floor of the Crillon. I was vouchsafed an appointment, was shown to a chair in an ante-room and asked to wait. A quarter of an hour passed, another and another and another. I was sitting, as it happened, close to the magnificent carved and gilt but not over-massive door that admitted to the great man. I could hear a murmur of talk interrupted by merry laughter, the flatter laughter of a male voice and the higher, more silvery laughter of a woman. I began to think I recognized this charming laugh and lo! at the end of an hour out came one of the prettiest and most frivolous of American Parisians, a little creature too silly to seem alarming but dangerously eager to make society capital of what she heard. Well; I was ushered in but was too furious at having been kept waiting for so long and for such a reason. The interview was frosty. When I told my friend of this result of his effort to put me in touch with the high-placed, he laughed and assured me that waiting around was the lot of the subordinate in all business whether public or private.

How glad I was that I had already passed the greater part of life having so little to do with either!

21

It is doubtful whether I could have made much headway in affairs, either public or private. I do not discuss the question of ability. What I do know is that I could never have hardened myself enough to use men and women as mere functions, as cogs in a wheel without regard to their own interests, their own personalities, their own souls. I might have been able to do so with a personnel I did not come in touch with, but I should have found it quite impossible to treat as mechanisms the people who were working with me in my presence, serving me as expert advisers, as secretaries, or mere typists. Even in our South and in Russia, masters could not help treating their domestic slaves and their house serfs more humanely than those they saw but seldom. My ideal would have been to be served in whatever grade of service, no matter how high or how humble, by people only who realized themselves completely by serving me. For my part, let me add, I have often thought that I, too, might have realized myself most completely, got the utmost out of myself, if I could have served an institution, a cause, best of all a person, who, by taking hold of my imagination, and offering fulfilment to my aspirations, absorbed me.

This leads me to confess to a dream that keeps returning in moments of undirected meditation. I dream of a society composed of individuals, each realizing himself entirely and the by-products of these realizations combining to make a civilization and a culture. There would be no prestige connected with one occupation rather than another. There would be no rewards. There would be thus no ambition to attain power and place. There would be no failures, no discontented, no brooders. My dream naturally excludes those who can realize themselves through violence only, or even through deliberate mischief-making. The last I should dispatch to far-away islands where they could enjoy each other's activities. The first I should assemble in two armies, and rely on their competitive spirit to develop enough animosity against each other to prevent them from uniting and becoming a danger to the rest of the community.

At times this dream takes shape so vividly, so clearly, and in such detail, that I could make a book of it. *Absit omen!* In this connection I may go on to confess that habitually I value activities more for what they do, for the physical and moral health of the individual, his group and community, and for the education—by which I mean chiefly the humanization of the individual and his society—than for the importance of the product, considerable, great even, though that may be.

Thus I encourage friends and still more disciples —if I may so distinguish young people who frequent me. I encourage them to pursue with zest what I see they are determined to do; what will on the one hand keep them out of mischief, keep them away from too much drink, too much sex, too much kicking their heels, too much picnicking; and on the other hand procure them the satisfaction that comes only from being engaged upon a task which seems to augment one's natural functioning. I do all I can to encourage them to feel that they are doing something worth while, something bearing a considerable relation to what their instinctive animal conceit inspires them to hope others will think of the result.

Needless to say I was as happy and proud as a father over a son's success if the achievement came up to expectation; if it did not, as was generally the case, and I showed but little interest in it, certainly nothing like the interest I showed previously, then the friend or disciple was disappointed, distressed; and nine times out of ten ended by turning to others for the admiration he required and for the ear to listen to his cock-crowing. That, by the way, is still another reason why I have lost friends, retained not many loyal disciples and got myself disliked.

Among the very dearest friends of our twenties were the two maiden ladies who under the name of "Michael Field" wrote in the 'eighties verses which attracted my attention while still an undergraduate. It was then my habit to spend Saturday afternoons at the Old Corner Book Store in Boston. There I found the latest novelties from London and one afternoon I picked up a small volume by this "double-headed nightingale" as someone dubbed the aunt and niece, and discovered a *Faun's Song* which charmed me. I recalled it vividly when I met them two or three years later in London, and told them so. I felt flattered when they assured me that Robert Browning liked the same poem. We made friends and saw more and more of each other. They joined us in Italy, travelled with us and made long stays with us in Fiesole. They already were suffering from the infection that took so many in the last decade of the nineteenth century: the urge to write plays, fervently hoping they would be staged. I saw it made them happy to get absorbed in their activities and in their dream of contemporary fame, honour, emoluments and turtle-eating. So I encouraged them to produce, and did not cold-douche their expectations. All the while these plays were getting worse and worse and were, I dare say, published at their own expense. As they appeared in print I managed, as luck would have it, to avoid saying what I really thought of them. Finally they brought out a rigmarole of the worst Elizabethan rant. It was about the widow of Crescentius and how she was to revenge herself on Otto the Holy Roman Emperor, her husband's slayer. The plot was of an indecency that only pure-minded, elderly, mid-Victorian virgins could have imagined; and the blank verse and the rhetoric would have filled with horror and indignation the worst understudies of Beaumont and Fletcher. This time the dear ladies would not be put off and wrote again and again, with more and more insistence, finally calling us "cowards" for not daring to tell them what we thought of this play of which they were so proud. We were in for it and I told them in as temperate language as I could muster, but tell them I did. Shortly a postcard arrived with the words: "All is not lost though Fiesole condemn. Vulgar journalists sail out of our lives." We did. For years we did not meet.

22

Yes, decidedly, what we now need as never before is not to work less, leaving far too much time for bored leisure, but work that is unproductive, leaves no results, leaves the morning as fresh as after the first dawn, and the evening as cool as when the Lord walked in the Garden. We produce more and more, more children, more machines, more goods, more printed matter, more painted canvases, more and more and more. Seeing that activity is as necessary to our health as breathing, we must study how to avoid transitive occupations and cultivate intransitive ones. I would encourage birth control not only in family life but elsewhere. I would impose a strict *numerus clausus* on the amount to be sown, the amount to be manufactured, the amount to be built, to be printed, to be painted, to be composed, etc., etc. In short I would apply anti-conceptionalism to all energizing. Not that I would reduce if I could the quantity of this energizing but I would turn it into unproductive channels, the channels of play, of song, of dance, of sport in various phases, always with reference to what it did to educate the mind, build up the body and humanize the individual and his group.

The Greeks did so to a degree never approached again. They tended in their best generations to turn everything into a sporting competition, even their politics. They put a value on words which turned them from slither, chatter, ejaculations, grunts, insults, and tam-tam invocations into poetry, into tragedy, into comedy, into oratory, into history. Life itself became a sport. Too good to last zoologically, but we still live on their example and thrive—even those of us, the vast majority of us, who have scarcely heard of them.

Some of their spirit survived, the ethical side only survived almost down to our own day, to account for what constituted "that superiority of the Anglo-Saxons" which seemed to preoccupy French thinkers of forty years ago. I do not recall their conclusions. To me it consisted in the phrase "playing the game." No metaphysics, no sanctions, but the imperative demand that as a gentleman you should accept the rules of society into which you were born and bred as a game you were to play fairly, with esteem for the opponent, with good humour, and with cheerfulness if you failed. Should this English spirit disappear under the stress of machines warring against men, then there would be little left of activities for their own sake rather than for the product; activities which among the ancient Persians and invading Teutons took the shape of feudal loyalty, which in the Middle Ages shone out as

Chivalry, which in the Spanish period took on the absurd but fascinating aspect of *punto di onor,* activities which in more recent times everywhere we called "soldierliness," which through centuries has been and still is one of the noblest and most glorious of human manifestations, the Catholic missionary the world over. He lives and dies for no utilitarian, no kind of material, not even a humanitarian, reason (although nobody so humane and so self-ignoring) but only and alone for the Glory of God. In him alone something, a reduced one-sided something, may survive of the intransitive activities of ancient Greece.

Many years ago I read a Hindustani tale turned into French by Garcin de Tassy (*Les Aventures de Kamrup,* Paris 1834, p. 105). Were there to be a call for a uniform edition of my writings, I should print this parable either as preface or epilogue. It runs like this: The hero of the tale is shipwrecked but manages to save himself by swimming to an island. The inhabitants see him come but will not let him land. They tell him that their island has no water and no food. Once a year a ship comes and brings the meat and drink required for the inhabitants, each receiving what is strictly necessary to keep alive, with nothing to spare. However, he succeeds in touching their hearts and they consent to receive him, everybody reducing his ration toward keeping him going. There he remains till the annual ship arrives with the supplies it brings, and takes away in payment the corals and pearls fished up by the islanders in the course of the year. The ship at first refuses him passage but, yielding to the prayers of the people eager to get rid of him, lets him embark on one condition. It is that no matter what he sees he must ask no questions. If he does he will be thrown overboard. He consents and they sail away. They sail and sail and at last they stop. To the passenger's amazement they begin to throw overboard the corals and pearls brought away from the island. He gets wild with curiosity, and, no matter what the consequences, he must ask and find out why they are acting in such a strange and wasteful way. They assure him that they will throw him to the devouring fishes but will answer him first: "Know that numberless islands are scattered over the seas and God, who provides for everything, will not let them starve. Some of them have no corn nor the least game upon which to feed. It is our task to freight vessels in the fertile islands with provisions. These once a year we carry to those that need them. We distribute to the barren islands under our charge the rations they need. On the same day of each year we draw up to their shores and hand them out supplies. But as we have no interest in keeping what they give us in exchange we throw it into the sea."

The world does not behave like the indifferent scavenger with the products of our labour. If they are nourishing and palatable it feeds them but remembers them no more than the loaf or joint digested yesteryear. Our creations, unless we are supreme geniuses, are destined to leave no trace even if they have their infinitesimal effect. Nothing

comes into being that leaves the universe unaltered, but your name will not, cannot survive. Not only were there kings before Agamemnon but poets, thinkers, mighty inventors. Who recalls them, and how long will our celebrities survive, even the most celebrated? A thousand, two thousand, three thousand, four thousand years, even as mere names empty of warm associations? So dream not of being known to posterity.

23

Perhaps the reasons I have tried to give for being less popular than I expected may be among those that prevented my ever feeling that I was "in it," that I belonged, belonged as a matter of course, in any community or even any country or nationality. Perhaps if I had lived on in Boston I might have ended by being a good Bostonian. As a matter of fact until quite recently the word "home," in so far as it meant a place and not a person or persons, invariably brought to my mind the New England capital. As it is I cannot recall since early manhood feeling more than on the margin of any group that I approached or that suffered my presence. I have had hundreds of moments of regret, of distress even, because I was not flesh of the flesh and bone of the bone of people. I have had as many moments of satisfaction that I was free to go where I liked, to keep what company attracted me, to advocate what causes appealed to me, to entertain what ideas amused me, without the fear of disappointing expectations or betraying loyalties. How well I remember Paris when the Dreyfus madness was raging. No Frenchman was allowed to be lukewarm, to use his reason, to consider the facts. He had to take sides. Certain strangers, I regret to say Americans in particular, in order I dare say to prove to themselves how much they were "in" with the best society, outdid the absurdest of the society's real members in their conduct over the "affaire." The few moderates on either side did not hide their envy that I could frequent both parties.

I have had no use for those recent versions of the savage's "man's houses," now called clubs, and have never belonged to one. Visiting, I was put up in some of them, particularly in America, although I fancy never in the smartest. I cannot recall, for instance, being made a temporary member of the Somerset or the Knickerbocker, but I remember to my great amusement being offered the hospitality of the Viennese Jockey Club. Those to which I had admittance I frequented with little pleasure. They were so intimate that they smelt of the nursing bottle, so much was the talk of babies and "little ones"; while the use of none but pet names was as effective in making one feel an outsider as in the highest circles of Austria-Hungary.

I am old enough to have survived contemporaries whose biographies have already appeared and whose correspondence has been published. I was scarcely surprised to note how little place I took in their lives, at least how little of it appeared to the biographers; but saddened somewhat discovering as

I did how little I inspired their subjects as letter writers, those particularly whom, like Henry Adams, I drew out so much in talk.

While they were alive I occasionally got the sense of being excluded, or rather not admitted to inner secrets. I do not refer to family secrets or group secrets. I was never keen about knowing these. But this sort of thing I would hear my elders say: "It is not our national policy." I would eagerly ask: "But what is our national policy? Who, what individuals, what junta possesses its secrets? Where can I find it stated, who will tell me?" Silence. Yet it must exist, for scores of times I have heard it appealed to in talk, and hundreds of times in print.

On the other hand I have never in England, let alone in America, come into a room where the abrupt stopping of talk made me feel as if I had surprised a group of conspirators, in this case plotting for their own against other countries with the felonian intent of depriving others of their own advantages. This happened to me numberless times in the European continent, in the so-called "Latin" countries particularly.

In this last connection there would be much to recount if I were putting down all of significance that I remember or could call back. Not here! Not now! Not yet!

24

I have dwelt so much on why I failed to gain the popularity I should so greatly have enjoyed, yet scarcely too much—unless indeed I am suspected of a certain complaisance, a complaisance hard to escape—if it goes, as in my case I trust it does, with a tendency of the mind to trace the difficulties, the ill will, the malignancy I encounter on my path as in great part if not wholly due to something in myself, something that I want to isolate and analyze, with the object of retaining the good and doing my utmost to reject the rest. It is not easy, for I flare up with indignation and can be only too vehement in resentment. I do try to understand why, and do not want like a child to blame it all on the piece of furniture against which, in his impetuous expenditure of energy, he barked his shins.

What a "liberal education" it would be to Japanese and Italians, Irish and Spaniards, French and English, what a world of good it would do, how it might alter international relations for the better, if they established highly respected committees out of their own midst to study why they were disliked by other nationalities. And the same as between class and class, between trade and trade, between individual and individual. It would have a humanizing effect on the rich if they got to understand why the poor hate them, and hate them most when, turning philanthropic with disciplined high condescension but no Christian charity, they try genuinely enough to better the lot of the poor by attempting to raise their standard of life. It would do much for our bankers who for ten years before the smash of 1929 were the admiration of the world as well as of their fellow-citizens and themselves if they discovered why, almost overnight, they were regarded as criminal lunatics, source and cause of all our mishaps and distresses. If the Spanish clergy would learn why their flocks once every while turn and rend them, burning churches, monasteries and convents, massacring priests, friars and even sisters of charity. If the grandees and hidalgos could stop to inquire why *los R-r-r-o-j-j-o-s* (as I have heard it expelled from pretty Spanish mouths fuming with hot hate), why these "reds" bore such resentment. If and if and if, what a better world it would be than the present one, when most of us childishly rush to pounce upon others as the mischief-makers, and never conceive that we ourselves may have been to blame. Human nature being what it is, we cannot expect that people will cry, "We all are miserable sinners" and embrace each other with tears, as I, had I had my way, should have approached the Germans on the Armistice Day of the last war. A change of heart is scarcely to be expected soon but a change of mind might bring it about in time. Only that the change of mind would have to result from inquiring first into what were the other fellow's grievances, and then why he clung to them. Aware of these two, you could argue with yourself in the first place to the extent that you suspected he was right, and with him to the degree that you hoped to persuade him he was wrong.

February, 1941

PART TWO

1

A friend of ours is a graphologist. She is unprofessional, but yet serious in her art. I know too little about it to overcome scepticism and to cease questioning how it operates. There can, however, be no doubt about this lady's sincerity. My handwriting left her puzzled. It was of a person who ought to have achieved much more than I have.

I was not surprised and still less shocked, for as I have been trying to say in the previous pages, I am haunted by a sense of failure. It is not due to vaulting ambition. So far as I know myself I have had little if any hankering for place, or lust for power. I was keenly aware of how enslaving both were. I had scarcely any competitive impulse.

I did not care about passing examinations. I was not elated when at Harvard to pass as high as possible in Sanskrit under Lanman, nor depressed because I got a mediocre mark in psychology.

I had taken the course under William James and attended it with the most zestful interest, not only listening open-mouthed to the exciting lectures of the professor, but doing the reading he recommended. Examination time came and a fellow student more devoted to sport and jollifying than to study begged me to help him pass it. I helped him so well that he got an A. As for me I got a C or at most a B, a result which confirmed my belief that it is the examiners who should be examined. I guessed what had happened. My listener had learned just enough to answer the questions in a straightforward, rudimentary fashion; whereas I probably elaborated, interpreted and bored the overworked and vexed examiner. I told James of this. He laughed grimly and shook me by the hand.

Having mentioned Lanman, I must ask permission to jot down a few anecdotes regarding him that have stuck in my memory. He was the best teacher of languages, or of any teachable subject, that I ever encountered. It was, however, at the expense of a total absorption in the grammatical side of his subject, namely, Sanskrit. He was justly proud of a reader in that language he had recently published and challenged us, his pupils, to find a single error, offering five dollars for every one we discovered. I did find one, a short for a long I, but never got the five dollars. Instead, many a supper of oysters and dry sherry after long evenings spent in the perusal of the *Mahabharata,* he supplying the vocabulary and disentangling the constructions when either was wanted. I recall interrupting to express admiration of a sloka just read. He looked up at me with bovine brown eyes and an expression of mingled surprise and distress at such a frivolous interlude. On the other hand, he intoned the *Tat savitur varenian* of the *Rig-Veda* with a fervour that must have meant something even if it only echoed his great teacher, W. D. Whitney.

Years passed without my seeing Lanman. The last war interrupted the life I had been leading and, besides, my own fifties inspired a backward look. So many I had revered and loved had gone, James Toy, Clymer, Wendell, J. H. White. Lanman was still among the living. He had grown deaf, I was told. Sure enough, he could scarcely hear a word I said; and I failed in my purpose, which had been to make him talk about Sanskrit studies in recent years, and his own part in them. I had scarcely sat down in his sanctum when he put his hand on a printed or typed sheet and with the utmost vehemence of indignation pushed it to me to read. He left me no time to do so, but spluttered out that it was a statement prepared by the president and fellows of Harvard informing every professor how much each of his pupils cost the university. As few students take up Indian languages, the cost of each seemed enormous. I confess to sharing a little of his feeling, only that in my case it was not so much rage as despair. To think of reducing a scholar's, perhaps a creative scholar's, a pioneering scholar's, value to the university, to America, to civilization, to a question of the money each of his pupils cost the corporation! Lanman went on, "But I cost them nothing. My chair is endowed, and endowed because its founders knew well enough that the subject could not be a popular one to be paid out of current college income."

I have forgotten the very alphabet of Sanskrit and it occurs to me to regret the youthful energies spent on trying to learn it as well as other marginal or exotic languages equally forgotten. They did discipline me, not only as an undergraduate but for years afterwards, rousing curiosities eager to be satisfied, curiosities which are not yet spent. But in the human lot there is no more gain without loss than loss without gain. What I have gained is not only the possibility of keeping up, to the extent of my leisure, with results of research in various fields; but immunization against humbug. The person of general culture has no idea how much he is misguided by fanatical propagandists and sheer fakers who claim or pretend to inform him about things of the Moslim or Hindu world. An acquaintance with the grammar of their languages opens an insight into their categories of thought, an even slight familiarity with their literatures in the originals, with their modes of feeling, and of course a direct contact with their arts, of the world as they desire it and want to see it.

Glad enough to enjoy these benefits, I yet cannot help regretting that I did not concentrate my energies upon Greek.

I ought to have been a Greek scholar. I do not mean a grammarian but a student of Greek letters, thought and art in all their phases through the twenty centuries of their vigour. I should have been happier that way; for always has everything Greek, in literature and art, had a fascination for me. It began from the moment I started to spell out Xenophon or look at a Greek statue even when accessible in cast only. I have regretted that I never learnt to read Greek fluently and carefree, without feeling obliged to analyse and parse and explain every iota subscript; for we were taught Greek not for its own sake but as a mental exercise for all and as a philological training for the few. The result is that nobody learns to peruse Greek as he does French or even German. Then ravenous curiosities led me far away from the Elysian fields, prevented my concentrating on Greek, and finally reduced me to spelling out Pindar and Æschylus with the help of a crib. I remain a wistful lover of Greek, a person of whom the most magnificent of recent Hellenists prophesied when he said that soon the only people to take pleasure in Greek would be those who could read it with the help of a translation. As for Hellenic visual art, it never palls. I can now look at the masterpieces only of European art from the Carolingian period to our own day. Yet I can be indulgent to the humblest and even meanest product of Greek art. I retain a voracious appetite for its shapes, its compositions, its narrative, its atmosphere—its world in short.

As a schoolboy I felt more at home in the streets of Athens than in those of Boston, which I knew so well. No history then known to me, not even of the battles of Lexington and Concord and Bunker Hill, seemed so near, took such hold on my imagination as that of Greece. Even in its jejune moments it fascinated me, and when I came to read it fluently in Herodotus my happiness was great. To this day nothing refreshes me so much, when I get fed up with Trobriand manners and customs and their not very divergent parallels in our midst, as turning back to almost anything Greek.

I know that their art, their literature, their written history even, offer no picture of Greek actuality. How sordid and foul, malignant and wicked it was I know from many sources, but chiefly from Jacob Burckhardt's cruel *History of Greek Civilization*. All the more admirable that they could aspire to a way of being so radiant, so beautiful, so vitally and deeply human.

2

Having mentioned just now Burckhardt's *Greek Civilization* let me express my regret that neither that nor his *Constantine*—the best still, a century after its publication—nor his *Reflections on the History of the World,* have ever appeared in English.* Indeed it is deplorable that except in the fields of theology and pure science the most thoughtful books in German seldom get translated.

3

Ranke confessed to Mommsen that he was urged on to his studies and researches by sheer curiosity. His curiosity resulted in scores upon scores of valuable publications—as valuable as any for their account of political events and their significance. My ravenous reading of history has remained sterile. Was it indolence, was it mere self-indulgence? I suspect that there are other reasons as well. One is that I felt responsibility to the printed word, realizing early that, once printed, a statement can never be effectively retracted and that errors, the more striking and "original" they seem, the more likely are they to appeal than reasonable statements. *Litera scripta manet* was an adage when writing by hand alone existed. How much more so now that the press can spread one's errors, one's rash judgments, one's hasty conclusions broadcast with no way of calling them back.

In talk we can modify instantly what seems to affect the interlocutor as we do not want him to be affected. Besides, talk runs away like water,

* Burckhardt's *The Age of Constantine the Great* and *Force and Freedom,* Reflections on History (Pantheon Books), were published in English in 1944 and 1949 respectively.

and even if some remains, most of it evaporates and one can hope that one's misstatements and exaggerations and false appreciations will not be recalled too clearly.

"It is the speech of the man who knows that is alive," says Plato in his *Phædrus,* "the written word is really but its ghost."

Wherefore, I refused to write on any subject outside my own, as already noted, shop, and even then never touched pen or paper until the confidence came that I knew all that just then could be known about the theme I was handling; and all that could be done with the more limited, more archæological part of my studies.

The same reasons made me hesitate, but naturally to a much greater degree, to write on the more general aspects and problems of art, some of which never cease tormenting me. How make sure of just what one meant? Assuming that you did by miracle attain such security, how find the words and phrases that would precisely and adequately communicate your meaning to others? At this point a discouraging, paralysing scepticism regarding the written word would overwhelm me.

I can scarcely recall when I did not deplore the inadequacy of words to communicate what we feel, or think, or even know. We believe the great poet says what he feels and thinks and that he goes beyond, and tells and teaches what we ought to feel and think. What he, the genius, feels and thinks and yet cannot express in words that satisfy him, of that we know nothing. Himself with time

—perchance after a short interval—reads what he has written and is pleased, forgetting how much it was in the nature of a desperate dash or last hope, a nebulous sketch of what was in his mind and heart.

Nobody knows all and exactly all that he means; not only no poet, no man of letters, no philosopher, no man of science, not even the mathematician. There is more in every one of us than he or even the greatest genius can express in words. We are driven to music, to song. We are in the position of the young woman who getting impatient with a stammering suitor, cried out: "If you can't say it, sing it!"

We use and abuse metaphors, images and comparisons, myths, wise saws, proverbs, as familiar references, and hope they will speak for us. There are more efficient instruments of communication than simple words and phrases that have to be learnt far more deliberately. This acquisition is culture, and a communal culture is the chief requisite for expression. That is one of the reasons why classical antiquity and our Middle Ages from 1200 to 1350 had such outbursts of literature and art.

Words are so unfit for exact statement that mathematicians are abandoning them, and other men of science tend to do the same. Lawyers would gladly follow them. As they cannot, they do the utmost to say exactly, precisely, and, as they hope, incontrovertibly what they have to put down in black and white. All the same the treaty, the contract, the document they draw up is no sooner signed than its interpretation is put in question, and litigation begins.

Philosophy indeed may be a product of disease in semantics. Most of it since Plato and Aristotle consists in attempts to interpret predecessors and then to interpret the interpreters. So of course is the pearl of the oyster. In the case of Kant, what a procession of commentators, each more burdened than the last not only with the effort of explaining the master but also the glosses and criticisms of intervening authorities. Likewise with Hegel and no less with our own contemporary, Bergson.

It is this feeling of the almost despairing inadequacy of words to render our meaning that led to phenomena like the vacuous glossolaly and the labyrinthine privacy of the ageing James Joyce. Indeed, may not many Americanisms and much American phraseology be due to the loss on the part of so many of us of the remains of the English vocabulary, as well as to the flattening out of idiom due to the carelessness and ignorance of natives, not to speak of the recent arrivals whose mother tongue is not English even when they are born in the United States?

"In the struggle against death all the arts and sciences have their roots," said Saint Gregory of Nyssa. So we may say that in the struggle against aphasia lie the roots of all efforts at verbal communication. Pathological aphasia consists in a discord between what the patient wants to convey to others and what he succeeds in conveying. Andrew Lang has the story of a ghost who like all ghosts suffered from aphasia. It was of one who, wishing to retrieve the fortunes of his bankrupt descendants by pointing to the treasure that lay buried under the family castle, could come no nearer to saying what he meant than driving around it on a hearse.

The French, it is true, have persuaded themselves and others that they succeed in saying just what they mean. They boast in their rudimentary grammars that what is not clear is not French. No doubt, but at what cost! At times they come near to pouring out the bath before it has washed the baby; or, to change the metaphor, to trimming the tree of all its flowers and fruits so as to give a clear view of its structure; or, after the habit of Procrustes, to cut the occupants down to the size of the bed. Clearness is too dearly bought at the price of ignoring all sorts of doubts, questionings, modifications, penetrations, etc., etc., that in many subjects, seriously regarded, will not submit to the schematic alembication required for simple statement. By which I do not mean to impugn the French gift, multiplied by tradition and training, for lucid exposition wherever possible. But almost nothing that is qualitative and ultimate in the human universe will submit to that kind of treatment; and although one may suffer acutely from German obscurity and English uncouthness one's more intellectual hankerings find food if not satisfaction in German and English rather than in French thought. A fanatical cult of clearness may kill not only philosophy but poetry as well; and to such a degree that in poetry recent France has taken refuge in hermeticism, that is to say in deliberate obscurity of expression. Indeed no little of French fashionable thought flirts with the various infantilisms described by André Thérive in his *Péché de Bêtise (L'Homme et le Péché, Présences,* Plon, Paris 1938). Rejuvenation will not come that way to the French. As for those who can never resist French literary novelties, hermeticism emasculates them.

On the other hand we must not accuse of insincerity the seekers for freer, fresher (I mean less used up), fashions of speech. They are all serious, even overearnest with regard to expressing themselves more completely. The author of *Poliphilo,* Rabelais' student from Limoges, the Marinists, the Gongorists were not looking for the obscurity of impenetrable forest shadow. They were bursting with eagerness to communicate a reality of their own and were sincere about it but almost as aphasic as the ghost in Andrew Lang's story. With goodwill and application we can descry what they had in their hearts and minds. We must learn to penetrate and get beyond the fog of words, not only in the word we read but in the word we hear, the word of even our familiars—let alone of friends or mere acquaintances. Not that we suspect their veracity or their best intentions to be truthful, but that we doubt their ability to say what they would want to say, what they mean to say. We must not be verbotoxic and allow ourselves to be too much affected by words. It is advisable, however, to avoid frequenting people who are verbalists chiefly, with whom discussion degenerates to argument and argument to a heated and not always fair run for the last word. Let us avoid being like Xerxes whom Herodotus reports as saying, "Then be well assured that a man's spirit dwells in his ears; when it hears good words it fills the whole body with delight but when it hears the contrary thereto it swells with anger." Words and all verbalism are cheques drawn against deposits of facts that must not be exceeded.

Because we are so verbotoxic, the word is mightier than the thought, and the pen mightier than the mind. Look not only at poetry but at any proposition written down. While thinking it over, it seemed doubtful and subject to reserves, attenuations, modifications. Once in black and white it becomes both adequate and convincing. If you read the same over after years, having meanwhile forgotten how precarious was the idea at the time, you may even wonder at the maturity and clarity of your thought so long ago.

My distaste for writing could have been encouraged had I been acquainted with the following passage that I have just read for the first time in Plato's *Epistle VII*: "Every serious man in dealing with really serious subjects carefully avoids writing. Whenever one sees a man's written composition these are not his most serious works, if so be that the writer himself is serious." Besides, I have always felt that I could not muster an elaborate vocabulary. I seldom read anything which does not impress me with the variety and luxuriance of its vocabulary. For years past I have made lists of words but never succeeded in assimilating and using them as if really mine. This feeling hinders if it does not prevent me from attempting to describe what I see, to express what I feel. Thus I have taken walks above my house hundreds upon hundreds of times, yet on no two occasions does the landscape look the same. The distances are milky or silvery or pearly or golden yet ever varied and I hail every shade of difference as if I had never seen its like. So with the trunks and stems of the trees I pass. Their winter coats of jade and malachite, the tawny, russet and gilt bronze foliage of the oaks are never the same. Little escapes my eye, but I can communicate scarcely any of it with the few and clumsy epithets at my disposal. If only I were like Adam who named the animals, roaming, creeping, flying, swimming, over the earth, in the water or in the air; or like Solomon who could name all the flowers in the field!

The nebulousness, the imprecision of words is well illustrated by the difficulty of translating from one language into another. It is hard enough to find equivalents between words implying some thing like the same concept and epithet in the three or four languages many of us are acquainted with, English, German, French and Italian. Look for instance at a book like J. G. Anderson's *Le Mot Juste,* an Anglo-French lexicon with verbal illustrations, (London, Dent). It will startle you out of your complaisance if you supposed you could find real equivalents in these two languages so close to each other that perhaps the majority of words in each has the same roots. It is, on the contrary, almost axiomatic that the nearer two words are to each other in French and English the less likely are they to mean the same thing. When one comes to German and attempts to translate its abstract and qualitative terms the task is fraught with almost insurmountable difficulties, as the English or French or Italian versions of German poets and philosophers prove amply. Yet, though many of us have a living contact with German and can consult friends belonging to that language group to help us out, who can offer a contemporary satisfactory rendering of *Gemüt?* When it is a question of Greek—Plato for instance—how convey in any speech of to-day the exact meaning of *Sophrosyne?* Then dare to translate the ancient Chinese and Indian thinkers.

To return from these considerations to myself and my doubts, hesitations and despairs about writing, I must not fail to add the following. I have always scribbled with the idea of helping myself to find out what I was thinking, and to clarify this thought, to give it shape satisfactory to myself. I have addressed myself, as I said earlier, to an internal interlocutor and never thought of the reader, the kind of reader I wanted to understand me. It is true that the writer of history or criticism in English is expected to address himself to a general public. In that case what the author wants to say should be put clearly, attractively, and persuasively. I never thought of attempting this, and failed accordingly, succeeding only by rare accident.

4

My task as a writer has not been facilitated by the circumstance that I have lived most of my life away from English-speaking communities. Although I have never learnt to speak French, German, or even Italian well enough to express myself correctly and agreeably in any of them, and because of that have often kept silence when I should have had plenty to say, yet, obliged to speak these languages and to read them even more, I have lost the fine certainty which I once may have had about the meaning of words and the use of idiom in English. From our point of view it is selfish of the French to refuse to speak any language but their own. Time and time again I have discovered that a French friend with whom I had to talk in his own tongue, even when my flow of speech was manifestly flagging, spoke fluent and nearly perfect English. Selfish of them, but it is the only way to preserve mastery over your own instrument of communication.

To all this must be added that frequenting authors, as I did from my earliest manhood, did not encourage me to be one of them. Now, as an old man, I read Plato and discover that his conclusions with regard to them do not differ from mine except in this. He believed that they, as indeed all artists, are little better than idiots, and that the muses enjoy selecting the silliest of all to be their mouthpiece. I would not go so far by any means, but a good part of the way I could not help following him. Many are the instances I could cite and characterize, and although in this place I want to avoid reminiscences, I may allow myself two examples.

I have already mentioned the aunt and somewhat younger niece who versified and playwrought together under the name of Michael Field. The aunt was a goat cropping in the garden of the muses while the niece was sensitive, intellectual, even intelligent and endowed with taste and judgment. Yet it was the aunt who had the gift, and the niece furnished the themes alone.

The other example is George Moore whom I frequented not a little in the first ten years of this century. I enjoyed his Irishry, his absurdity, his malice, his anecdotes about Yeats, Hugh Lane, A.E., and other countrymen of his, not to speak of acquaintances and friends we were seeing together in London and its coasts. He was so silly in judgement of people, so uncritical about books and pictures, so ignorant, so anti-intellectual, so vulgarly vituperative against religions in general and Roman Catholicism in particular, that his performances frequently became a circus and especially so when his brother the Colonel was present. Yet when *Ave, Salve* and *Vale* came out I felt humiliated not to have perceived previously what a gift Moore had as a writer. Later, when I perused his imaged tapestry narratives, first *The Brook Kerith* and then his *Héloise and Abélard,* I had to realize that the pen is mightier than the thought, the learning, the feeling, the understanding; and that the muse of muses, Style, had chosen this up-to-date stage Irishman for its mouthpiece. Just because he was all I have said he could approach the subject matter of both these romances with the wisdom and, let us add, the beauty that comes from the mouths of babes and sucklings.

5

Other failings I could confess in numbers if I had the patience to relate them and could count on anyone to hear me through. So I will not attempt to give further reasons for dissatisfaction with myself—they might end by seeming more boastful than penitential—except to return to the feeling I have that I have never been what is or used to be called a "good fellow." I return to it because I believe that now in my old age I can account for it. I seem to remember that I had little if any of the instinct so universal in mankind, the play instinct, the love of make-believe and pretending-to-be that makes up almost the entire life of the child and never quite leaves us even in our greyest maturity. Only, as we reach full manhood, it gets harder and harder to give vent to this instinct when we are alone by ourselves, and easier and easier to enjoy it in company. So old alumni and all sorts of ex-service men come together periodically to pretend and make believe that they are still adolescent, with futures before them and not behind them, boasting of what they have done and will do and lying communally in a way that distressed me because, prig that I was, I did not realize that it was all play, nobody taking the cries of self-adulation as more than a way of jollifying by looking back to the time when it was so glamorously pleasant to look forward.

The very exaggerations should have put me on the scent and made me indulgent. A Fourth of July toast rises from the depths of my memory as an example. It was something like this: "I drink to my country bounded on the north by the aurora borealis, on the south by the precession of the equinoxes, on the east by primeval chaos and on the west by the Day of Judgement."

Not that in my youth I was not a bit of a *mythomane,* the word by which the French politely designate a person who does not make too searching an inquiry into the historicity of the facts he is relating whether they concern others or himself. I even tried to pretend to what I was not; but failed with myself if not with others because I could never for the briefest instant cease to be aware of facts and abandon myself to a myth or pretence.

I cannot take part in any ritual, whether religious, civic, or merely social. I can only stand aside and enjoy it, admire it, or criticize it as an art performance.

So, apart from the game of games, the game of life itself, of life never losing its quality of an adventure over seas and into lands still to be explored and charted, I have not enjoyed to even a small degree personating what was not my ordinary self—theatricals, masquerading, or dancing. I was not even as Hume to whom pleasure meant "whisk and disputation." I could get no enjoyment out of cards. Having no competitive impulses, I was annoyed to see how it upset people to lose. When I had to play, I could cheat to make others win—small sums naturally. So not caring for "whisk," I had only disputations left, but of them great was my enjoyment.

Yet my distaste for convivial occasions was not merely priggish, unless indeed what I am going to say is tantamount to priggishness. It is this.

The most inalienable possession I know of is my own reason, as well as confidence in the reason of every other individual to whom reason can be attributed. Everything that tends to diminish one's command of this faculty alarms me, and whatever deprives us of it altogether horrifies me and fills me with loathing. I grant that ecstasy, whether spiritual—if that word has more than verbal meaning—æsthetical, or even merely physical, does likewise deprive us of reason. Ecstasy, however, of the higher sort is not below but above and beyond reason; and rare are the cases when its inactuality can do harm; its duration is so brief. But the submergence of reason under the threshold of awareness which takes place in gatherings and banquets that tend to intoxicate before the participants have drunk much is something I preferred not to submit myself to, and failed to enjoy as an event. Needless to add, that more distressing still to me was out-and-out drunkenness. Shall I confess that among the many considerations that led me to prefer Florence and Italy to Boston and America, to London and England, as a residence, was the recollection of reeling, whisky-smelling men and women, dead-drunk with babes in their arms that one encountered the moment one left the genteel quarters of Anglo-Saxon towns.

It follows that I no less disliked another result of intoxication. It is de-individualization. No doubt this accounts for my incurable anti-militarism. Everything about soldiering works for mechanizing and automatizing the individual—or this was the case till the so efficient German army in the present war, which, I am informed, is based on small units leaving much more room for the tactical initiative of the individual corporal and sergeant. Whatever may happen in the future when, likely enough, the soldier will disappear altogether before the engineer, the mechanic, the electrician, up to the present the soldier has helped on the humanization of mankind despite himself only because of the unpremeditated, even unimagined, consequences of those of his activities that happened to be good. Except as spearheads of blind forces—blind although employing and involving human agencies—the military mind, the military leader, has been of little help to mankind on the hungry, thirsty, sore-footed, weary march to the invisible Promised Land, He lends himself, it is true, to the verbal artist as a life-enhancing subject for epic narrative. That aside, I can think of George Washington only as serving his country equally well in peace as in war. Can the same be said of Alexander, of Caesar, of Napoleon, of Moltke? It was the last named who would have marched on Vienna after Sadowa, who insisted on the annexation of Alsace Lorraine after Sedan. We have had our President Grant and the Germans their Hindenburg. God save us from their like and their hell-paving good intentions.

PART THREE

1

I dare say that when young and still an undergraduate I read Cicero on old age and later Cornaro. I recall nothing of either. I approach the subject with little if indeed anything taken over from others. I know that I do not escape the law of averages even when I feel unassociated and unrelated; nor do I flatter myself that I shall say things that have not been said before. On the contrary, there is no feeling, no thought of mine, that could not be paralleled innumerable times here, there and everywhere. In fact it is the reason why I think it worth while to write about myself. In a modest way I am a representative figure and no mere freak, as Friedrich Hebbel said of himself when charged with lacking originality.

Twenty years ago, when I first suspected the approach of old age, I thought it would be interesting not only to observe but to keep record of its manifestations and symptoms. It is a pity that my pen-shyness got the better of me. I had dispositions for doing it, for I was not afraid of getting old. Not only not afraid, but not rebellious, not indignant, not outraged. I have kept these poisons for what I fancied, imagined, or felt convinced, sincerely convinced, could be prevented. Natural processes, even natural catastrophes, storms, floods, tidal waves, earthquakes, volcanic upheavals —these one can deplore but not be indignant with. Every evil, on the other hand, that might be avoided drives me wild and whatever evil is done by man seems to me still as something that need not have been permitted. We pay heavily for having eaten of the Tree of Knowledge and learning thereby to distinguish between good and evil. We distinguish by and through reasoning, and cannot forgive creatures endowed with that dearly bought commodity, reason, for refusing to use it or, still worse, for deliberately abusing it. There would be much to say in this connection but to say it as I would wish to say it would take too long and carry me further out of my course than even these helter-skelter pages can allow. I shall make but this one remark. I have sinned and despite myself continue to sin because I cannot yet get rid of the notion that man is capable of being entirely rational, if only he wanted to be. I have burned with the desire to induce him to be so and the Lord knows I have tried hard enough. The results were seldom satisfactory and for the most part led to estrangement or worse. For man, taken even as an individual and as the heir of all the ages and civilizations, retains an insoluble quantity of the irrational in his make-up. To be a "judge of men,"—as it is called, is to know what to allow to this element in each case, and how to circumvent it. As for men in the lump, the mass, they are about as rational as a drove of oxen or a stampede of buffaloes, and woe to him who tries to lead them by means of intelligible speech instead of brutish sounds and the skilful use of the lasso.

Conceited no doubt I am, but not to the extent of supposing that I am wholly rational. Indeed, what I have been saying about myself proves the contrary, and the description I now undertake of my present state of body and mind will be dashed, spotted and stained with irrational elements. In so far as they are purely physical I am not tempted to rebel against them. In the much vaster fields of the mind and soul I know by experience that it is useless to think of eliminating the undesirable irrational elements in one's view of things in general, and utterly impossible to improve what is called one's character.

So I was disposed to take the aches and pains that shyly, almost roguishly, began to peep through the cracks of the body not only with curiosity but good humour. I had always found the first touch of pain exciting and, up to the point where it was beginning to be acute, rather fun, as making me aware in a spot where I had hitherto been insensitive. It added to the empire of consciousness. Worse followed after a while, something worse than aches and pains. It was the increasing liability to fatigue. I still loved to walk fast, to run uphill, to leap from rock to rock. It took years before I yielded and learned to walk quietly, to climb little and to jump not at all. Of the last I was cured by landing on my heels instead of the ball of my foot after a leap of some twelve feet, and getting the backbone and ribs so shaken that for days I could not stir. After that I learned to step warily. And so with my eyes. For the first time they began to smart after hours of reading by artificial light, and resent daylight that was too fierce. The ears too refused more and more to make out just what people were saying when, as is too often the case, they all talk together and, in Europe, so frequently in different languages. It grew harder to catch the talk on the stage and I would make out little of a play at the beginning.

On the mental side it was no better. I began to notice that my mind was refusing to take problems by assault, preferring to sneak around and leave them unsettled—hoping they would be left far behind; that I avoided the consecutive, exact, geometrical thinking I used to do previously, little though that was; that I counted more on the kind of mental activity—passivity, rather—that may be compared to a shower of falling stars on a pitch-black night, or to an occasional comet trailing across one's inner sky. More and more did it tire me to concentrate on one subject, and I discovered that the length of time was getting shorter and shorter in which I could work without a back-ache, and without feeling as if the top of my head might fly open. It took years to convince me that it was not self-indulgent indolence but disability of spine and brain that would not let me energize as I used to. I was seventy before I gave up fighting and yielded to the necessity of diminishing my hours of work as well as of play, to know when to lay off before fatigue became acute, before I became overtired, and to relax physically and mentally.

"Overtired," a word that used to amuse us and at the same time to annoy us when the Michael Fields were travelling with us. My wife and I were in the late twenties and they considerably older. Now I was experiencing it myself. I scarcely knew what it meant to be consciously tired until, returning one day in October '89 from tramping up and down the ravines that furrow the countryside around Madrid, instead of feeling, as always hitherto after long walks, a delicious balm glowing in my veins, a numb ache possessed me. As the hours went by without bringing relief, I had time to inquire what was the matter and concluded it must be what I had heard of as "fatigue."

As this process advanced I began to be haunted by a feeling I had never had before, the feeling

of hurry. When it commenced I was nearing sixty and I had not experienced it before. I had never worried about work, for I always could find time for it, if not in the forenoon then in the afternoon, if not all day long then at night. I had been ever ready for a jaunt or a talk, always disposed for company, always eager for a voyage of discovery and better still of rediscovery, whether among people, books, sights, and sounds or a vague wandering aimlessly leading on and on and ever on to which I have given the name of "*Dahin*-ness." I need scarcely add that it is based on the word meaning "thither" in Goethe's *Kennst Du das Land.*

Let me interrupt and confess that before discovering hurry I had been made impatient to the point of exasperation by the nervousness and fussiness of friends over their writing, particularly if they were minor poets. Even major ones were not free from what used to impress me as unsocial and even unfriendly behaviour. Not only would the Michael Fields cut short whatever we were doing together but even such a productive as well as gifted artist as Edith Wharton would cancel at the last minute plans of meeting, of travelling, or worse still, interrupt them in mid-course, leaving us in the lurch because she suddenly had a fit of work come over her! I must on the other hand make it clear that apart from these exceptional annoyances she never fussed about her work, never made you feel that it obsessed her. Quite the contrary, even her familiars might have frequented her for years without discovering that she was a prolific and distinguished author. But the minor writers were always talking about their work and how they must waste no time, how they must isolate themselves, how they must hurry to get to their tormenting task. Women with child could not be more tiresome than these versifiers with a sonnet in their bellies.

That was seldom my case, but then I was not a creator. Toward sixty, however, I suddenly became aware of "time's winged chariot hurrying near" and of the fact that henceforth I must husband the hours, diminished as they have not only in quality of output but in quantity as well; reduced in numbers by the pressing need of more and more time for vacuous repose and idle day-dreaming.

So for some ten years I felt hurried, felt it in my bones, my marrow, my viscera. Hurry came near, killing the supreme joy, joy in the exercise of function, by making me worry about the time it would take to reach a result instead of letting it follow as the relatively unimportant by-product of so much mere living. No more browsing on books in out-of-the-way fields and remote corners, no more free-hearted conning of the classics for hours together if the mood seized me. I had planted a garden with nooks where I was going to sit and take pleasure in my favourite *Dichter*—I use the German word deliberately because our word "poets" implies verse, whereas Thomas Browne never wrote but in what we call prose, although nothing could be further from the prose current from Macaulay to Matthew Arnold that I was brought up on.

By the way, the prose of the last twenty or even thirty years, owing perhaps to the influence of a gifted Pole who could sing but not speak English, combined with the Yankee hanker for racy and unhackneyed turns of speech and imaged phrases, this recent American which is also colouring English prose, is getting to be more like Jacobean than any intervening prose that we have had. Ours is snappy and impudently familiar, while the other was solemn, vituperative and august. Theirs a lordly claret, ours a heady gin; both equally removed from water, milk and other unfermented or only slightly fermented drinks.

Returning to the garden I had planted, by the time it had grown and could be enjoyed, hurry seized me; and for the arbours and fountain curbs where I was to sit and listen to the nightingales, blackbirds, thrushes and larks, and draw in the fragrance of roses, lotuses, and lime blossoms I never found the leisure. I could only glance and pass on.

Leisure is youth's most blessed possession; no Pandora's box, but the bosom of Demeter where wax and ripen the fruits that refresh manhood and preserve it from sinking into brutishness, sanctimoniousness and philistinism.

Losing the sense of it was the most painful experience connected with approaching old age. I began to be avaricious of time, to begrudge the moments spent on exercise, to discard desultory reading, to abandon my Homer and Virgil and *Golden Treasury,* to find no free intervals for the Bible and for Shakespeare. I became anxious about the quarter hours as they slipped away, and would have stood at street corners hat in hand begging passers-by to drop their unused minutes into it.

Time goes faster and faster as we get older. It is conceivable that if one lived long enough, say one hundred and fifty instead of seventy-five years, time would cease to be, that is to say one would lose the sense of the lapse of time, of duration. The psalmist who tells us that to the Eternal a thousand years is but a minute does not poetize. He may understate a fact.

Fretting about time is due to a desire to achieve before it is too late. I kept telling myself that what a man can accomplish after sixty, unless he is one of those rare geniuses who, like Titian, creatively renew themselves into their seventies, eighties and even nineties, amounts to little more than coffee made with grounds, tea with leaves that have served again and again and again. The first brew gave off the specifically individual aroma that counts for newness and, in fortunate instances, for refreshment. After that our output gets thinner, more neutral, and serves little to keep us busy and to give us the illusion that we are not pensioners but still productive members of society.

For myself, so little faith have I in any work connected with art history I still could produce that for the present I have dropped a book I was writing on decline and recovery. Unable to live without shedding ink, I have taken to writing this which may interest others more than what I have been associated with hitherto, while at the same time helping me perhaps to understand myself better.

Saying this to myself for ten years and more, and facilitated no doubt by the sense of sinking vitality due to the piled-up years, has had the effect of making me almost indifferent to what I may still produce, and better still as to when it will be completed.

2

The future is a *pré-venant*—if I may venture to coin a French word—but as much of a vampire as any *revenant*. It has an adjectival, clouding, illusory, disturbing effect on the present. It is the source of our few hopes and many fears. But old age has no future, and we should accept and rejoice in this certainty, unless indeed we are haunted by the most invincible of all bogeys, the fear of death. The fear of death, as Hamlet concludes, is not so much the fear of ceasing to be, as the fear of what will happen if we survive. The greatest rebellion of mankind is first against the probability of annihilation, and then against the possibility of a thrice-wretched survival as at best encountered by Ulysses among the heroes in Hades and at worst in the hell of the Egyptians, made grotesque by Etruscans and monstrous by Christian belief, if not dogma. History has been studied from so many points of view! I should like to see it written as the rebellion against death and the belief in a hell. It would comprise more of human endeavour than any other approach, political, economical, or military. Little in the events of the historical millennia that has not been influenced, if not determined, by it. I wonder whether there is any other access to the past that would be more revealing and penetrating, more illuminating and educative. Strange, too, is the way these beliefs and fears have affected different peoples. Why, for instance, do the Israelites, as recorded in the Old Testament, betray so little interest in an after-life and no fear at all of what may happen if there is one? Why did the Nilotic fellah whose lot must have been as hard as any on earth, cling to life with such a greedy lust for its continuance? What made the Thracian—or was it his cousin the Scythian?—feel so sure of a future life that you could make a debt here to be paid there?

I have had no fear of death since my seventh year at latest. My grandmother died before I was five. Her departure stunned me. She had meant more to me than all other people put together, including my mother. I not only missed her day and night but could not understand what had happened. If memory does not play an absurd trick on me, it was during these difficult months that I had an incredible dream.

I dreamt that my grandmother was extended on a slab of black marble in a tomb-like chamber of polished black stone. She herself was encased like a mummy, and against the wall stood a number of Osirises like those we still see at Karnak in the Temple of Ramses III.

I cannot doubt the dream, and the time when I had it is most likely to have been when I still was haunted by the obstinate and unintelligible fact of my grandmother's death. And yet—at that time I could scarcely have heard of Egypt or if I had, it was a word that could have meant nothing to me. I could not have known anything about mummies or Osirises and least of all could I have seen pictures of hypogees. The only explanation would be that I must have had this accurately visualized dream when I was already conversant with Egyptian funeral rites and customs, and in after-memory transferred it to my earliest years. It is an explanation hard to accept.

Be that as it may, grandmother's death made me ponder and inquire. All I seemed able to learn was that after one died one went before awesome judges who assigned one to terrible punishments for sins. Were animals, too, subject to such treatment? No. Why? They had no souls. I envied the animals. When dead they were dead, and that was the end of it. Yes, death was the evil of evils. How could it be avoided? Stocks and stones do not die. Better then to be a stock or stone. But they have not lived at all. No, no!

Anything rather than not to have lived. With that utterly childish conclusion I was for ever liberated from the fear of death.

I was then at the "metaphysical age" of childhood and rediscovered for myself the questions that puzzled the pre-Socratic philosophers. A little girl was my dearest chum. The problem of death had a far more absorbing interest for her than for me, an interest almost urgent. She died in the midst of this, and left me feeling that it was unwise to think and talk about death.

Since then I have thought little and talked less about death. What can one think or say about a matter so unthinkable, only less unthinkable than after-life, a discarnate existence, or what you choose to call it? Our Maker has not given us the mind for conceiving such matters (except verbally), still less for understanding them.

What is strange is that although I am now well on in old age and perhaps at its last moments, accepting life as it is for worse as for better, accepting it, loving it, rejoicing in it, I feel no anticipated regret, let alone present rebellion at leaving it. Is it because I feel deep down that I am not destined to leave it, that nothing of me will remain that has not already been joyously offered to everybody and everything that survives me?

Subjectively one never dies. It is only objectively that we expect to depart this life. The subjective ego cannot conceive, except verbally, that he will cease to be. He is there when he thinks

of himself as dead, when he thinks of the earth falling into the sun, the sun disappearing into space, the entire universe wiped out. He cannot go further in annihilation, but if he could he would survive.

Believers in immortality are therefore justified in practice. They will never know that they have died, for during the very last flickers of consciousness they were alive.

We have got no further, we can get no further with the brain we have, than the Saxon thane summoned to discuss in the king's hall whether they should become Christians. The hall was brilliantly lit and a bird flew in at one window and flew out of another. The thane said, "Like this bird out of the dark, back to the dark we flutter after a moment in the light," and advised accepting Christianity.

What though if the promise has lost its interest, if we do not desire an after-life that we cannot imagine except as a fairy picture; if the myths of the various establishments are reduced to poetry; if their dogmas involve their justifying a train of thought that we can no longer follow because we cannot accept the premises out of which they should issue as the rivers of Paradise from the Garden of Eden and with logic absolute pursue their unswerving course to the sea of faith? What if their rituals are only a performance, sublime and more comprehensive than any other, but still a performance; if we no longer need their sanctions for conduct and if their morality is tainted with too worldly institutionalism on the one hand and on the other with unrealizable ideals of selflessness and even undesirable other-worldliness?

Chiefly I have Christianity in mind, though not to contrast it with any other religion that I prefer. On the contrary, I regard Christianity as the best and highest religion to which the white race could attain, so long as they must have institutional religion with a framework of dogmas and canopies and curtains of myth. Furthermore, among the Christians I greatly prefer the Roman Catholic and the Orthodox churches to the various sects that attempt to rationalize, to demythicize, depoetize Christianity, and yet wish it to retain its fundamentally magical essence.

The magical world—Spengler's happiest phrase—is a fairy world. I dwelt there for my first thirty years. It was hard to abandon it, to be driven out of Paradise even as our first parents were. Like them, as described by our sublimest poet, heir of all that is most noble and majestic in Israel, in Greece and in Rome, I looked back often and with what homesickness and heartsickness! But there is no return, any more than one can creep back into one's mother's womb, although it must have been so cosy there, so carefree, so comfortable.

So I regard myself as a Christianity graduate in the sense in which I am a college graduate. We Americans return to our alma mater on class days and pretend that we are boys again, not yet graduated but about to be so. Yet we do not think of returning to undergraduate life despite all its sweet alluring memories. I feel toward the Church the same gratitude, the same affection, the same admiration as I do toward the university. There is much on the institutional side of Harvard that is distasteful and a great deal more—incomparably more—on the institutional side of Holy Church; but I do not want the one abolished any more than the other. On the other hand, the Church, even as an institution, is measurelessly more wonderful than any university, than all universities put together. Taken as an historical entity, man-made though I hold it to be—indeed because man-made and subject to the frailties, greeds, and lust of the individuals who through the ages have composed it—there is no other creation of mankind to compare with it. It is humanity's grandest, completest, and most beautiful achievement.

3

I am tempted to launch out on my attitude toward institutions. It would take a book by itself even though I was as brief as I can be. This much I can say in a few lines; that I regard them, big or little, hoary with age or with their plaster still wet, as necessary evils. They can never be other. They exist to actuate ideas, desires and ideals. But they can work only through individuals, subject to their animal nature, each working for his own ease, his own safety, his own advantage, his own hopes, his own appetites, his own lust for power. They end therefore by subjecting everything to a common average, distorting and even falsifying the ideals they were to serve—as, for instance, the teaching of Christ and His Apostles. As for political institutions, it is enough to recall how quickly Mazzini changed into Mussolini or Schiller and Stein into Hitler *und Gefährten.*

Institutions are nevertheless as necessary to the functioning of any and every branch of human society as are the less noble parts of our bodies. We cannot do without bladder and intestines. Unable to get on without them, we see to it that they are kept in good order and function for the good of the body as a whole and not for their own pleasure, so to speak. Institutions are necessary evils of the same nature, and their activities must be carefully watched over so that they do not cease to serve us. Often I have heard the question: "What is liberty?" Liberty, I would say, is the right and duty to watch and ward over institutions, so as to keep them as obedient servants of the public and to prevent them, by criticism of the severest and most searching kind and by action if necessary, from growing to be the public's exploiters and tyrants.

Despite all that critics can say against the Church on its institutional side it remains, I repeat, the greatest and most commanding fact of our history. No thinking man, no matter what his private views may be or what creed or sect he adheres to, even if non-Christian, can fail to be aware of it daily and even hourly. He cannot escape its perspectives, its values—although these are seldom put in full practice by its members—nor its ideals, no matter how poorly realized. "European" and "Christian" are practically synonymous. Until recently, if now no longer, a European, in any part of the world not inhabited by other Europeans, would be taken for a Christian as a matter of course.

What Christianity, so fundamentally, so root-and-branch the product of our own Mediterranean-Atlantic civilization of the last three thousand years, may get to mean to other races is an interesting speculation. What on first contact it means to the heart of Africa is illustrated by a story General Count Adalbert de Chambrun told me. He had been with Brazzà in the French Congo, and was afterward military attaché in Washington during the Presidency of Theodore Roosevelt. Asked what effect Catholic missionaries were having on the Negroes, the general said: "Perhaps the story I am going to tell you will suggest an answer. One of the fathers was making good progress with the natives and felt particularly happy over the two sons of a chief. They seemed well on the way to becoming exemplary Christians. For some months he had to be away. When he got back he heard to his disappointment and grief that these young men had in the short interval forgotten his teaching and had relapsed into their cannibal practices. He called them and asked if it was true. 'No, Father, what you have been told is not true. We did return for a while to our tribe while they were fighting with their enemies. Some of them were killed and were being roasted. The smell was delicious and the temptation great but as it was Friday we abstained.' "

When Christianity made its first appearance beyond the sacred circle of ancient culture, its effects could not have been very different. It is enough to read the Gospel of the Infancy to see what a brute popular imagination made of the Christ Child. One wonders, by the way, what after eighteen centuries Christ means to our distinguished French contemporaries who boast that they are Catholics but not Christians.

Blessed are they born to a religious and political faith which their mature reason need not reject. I still speak of religion and politics as if they could be separated. It is a bad habit; for though they are different in origin and outlook, in moments of crisis they always have been and remain psychologically identical, equally irrational, passionate, and intolerant.

4

If I speak of myself as a Christianity graduate it does not mean that I have no beliefs remaining to guide and comfort me. I am still the religious person I always have been. I should be glad of heart to join in any worship, to partake of any sacrament whether Christian, Jewish, or Moslem, Buddhist, Taoist, or Shintoist, if I did not fear that thereby I was supposed to accept the literalness of their myths and the actuality of their dogmas. By graduating from myths no matter how sublime and dogmas architectured no matter how marvellously—as marvellously as the most majestically and subtly thought out of Gothic cathedrals—I seem to myself to have concentrated and intensified my faith. Faith in what? Faith in IT, and faith in Humanity.

Humanity first. I neither ignore nor forget what has been said against men and women singly and in the lump by Egyptian scribes, by Hebrew singers and prophets, by Greek poets and philosophers, by Hellenistic cynics, Christian Fathers and Doctors throughout the ages and by pessimists nearer our own day, among them "Frederick the Great" with his *"Er weiss nicht, mein lieber Sulzer, was für eine verfluchte Rasse die Menschen sind"*—You have no idea what a bad lot is mankind. And who that has not been wrapped in cotton wool from cradle to grave, living a sheltered life, has not been confronted by every kind of malignity, cruelty and spiritual squalor, not to speak of the meanness, the vulgarity, the childish shout of "me first" which one encounters on every hand, occasionally in one's dearest friends and more often still in one's own breast! I have moments of savage vindictiveness, happily of slight duration, when it is hard not to despair of the featherless bipeds that we are. Beginning with myself, we seem to differ from other wild beasts only by possessing mechanisms that make us a millionfold more destructive than the Siberian tiger that has only its leap, its claw, its tooth. Then I turn and recall not only the beauty, the loveliness, the charm that mankind shares with the wild and the tame animals, but the disinterested goodness that in humanity appears often enough to make us aware of what it can be and indignant at the too frequent, too barbarous indifference to these qualities. Instinctively we take for granted that we have got beyond mere animality, beyond cannibalism, and that we prefer good to evil and, what is more, that we can distinguish between them. We assume it to such a degree that we as instinctively believe that cruelty, malignity, deliberate wickedness are the exception. So much is this taken for granted that people who practise evil feel obliged to defend themselves. They try either to justify it on the ground that necessity knows no law or that their conduct, despite our inveterate prejudices and obstinate blindness, is dictated by a conviction that in the long run it will bring about a better world.

Man is a destroyer, but what a creator! The human past, long before written history begins, is strewn with figured records of his love of beauty and testimonials to his genius as creator. Indeed, man seems to have begun as artist and only in the last hundred years has he succeeded in emancipating himself from art completely, exchanging the possible Phidias in him for a Ford. This transmutation unhappily carries with it something that a mass-produced and mass-producing Ford does not think out. If he did, he would conclude that the Ford's destiny was to head the totalitarian state in its headlong course towards the complete mechanization of mankind. There is a chance that on even this unpromising path man may strew reminders of his invincible aesthetic sense, no matter how much like a genie imprisoned in the perfection of machinery.

With the invention of the Alphabet began that outburst of epics and lyrics and prophecies and apologues and histories which continues to this day, with less decline of energy and quality than any of the other arts have suffered, excepting perhaps music.

Music itself, the music of the last three centuries conjuring up with wordless sound audible edifices as sublime as any in architecture, disciplining, canalizing, clarifying our emotions, and transporting them into realms as remote from our brutish beginnings as our animal present will permit! On the wings of music we soar above and beyond nature, further than any other vehicle can carry us, where some distant day we may reach the limitless ecstasy of Infinitude.

I recall with awe, with rapture, with gratitude, the heroes, the saints, the creators who, starting with the humblest of us as furless, featherless, two-legged animals, have had the vision of ever better worlds and the genius to try to realize them. Compared with the rest of us they are gods. Nor are they deities who have to command worship. One cannot help adoring them. They console and comfort. They have been; they will be again. They are here now. Distressing and terrifying as is the hour we are so anxiously passing, mankind has gone through as bad, survived and advanced on its way to the still distant goal, its complete humanization.

When I was a lad of fifteen or so I read George

Eliot's essays as well as her poems. The *Choir Invisible* left me with a feeling of utter incredulity and the essays only strengthened my dissent. What, this creature, this biped, so feeble, so sinful, so ugly —for the looks of most men and women found so little favour in my boyish eyes—so quarrelsome, so noisy, so vulgar, this mankind worthy of worship, not aesthetic but religious worship! Nothing seemed more absurd, more far-fetched. Sixty years later I am as little disposed to join a positivist community (if any survive) to worship humanity with a set ritual and elaborate catholicizing practice. On the other hand, I now partake in the adoration of great men—needless to say not soldiers and statesmen and inventors only—and I discover in myself a fast-growing impulse to love the rest of our species so long as they are not out for evil-doing as an end. Indeed at the rate my spirit is now moving, I may live to include even the lovers of evil within the remoter radiations of my love.

Far from finding most men, women and even children ugly in the way I used to as a lad, a youth and as a young man, the greater number now look beautiful to me. For one thing, people under fifty now seem so young—smooth skins, bright eyes, well-proportioned figures, firm step. Perhaps I should not enjoy this continuous delight of the eyes if I lived elsewhere. Living as I do in Italy, and in Tuscany at that, I seldom go out of my villa without encountering young people as lovely as flowers, and beauty in all classes, among the peasants working in the fields, the soldiers returning to barracks, the small townspeople out for a stroll. And to see the youth of the countryside at harvest time makes one wish to be born again as one of them. They can be described only in terms of the Song of Songs which is Solomon's.

The normal mother seems unaware of the shuttling backward and forward of the little ones, their chatter, their questions, their quarrels, their petulance, their tears, their screams, their tumultuousness. Her love embraces everything about them. Real love is of that nature. I could have had little of it in my earlier and middle years. I had a horror of crowds, of human noises, of the life of the street and the fair, of public gardens, cafés, restaurants and even clubs.

Then some years ago, I remember, we were passing the autumn in Rome in the heart of what elsewhere would be a slum but in Italy was a street of noble palaces still shared by their titled inhabitants with common and even humble people. During the four and twenty hours of the day, few were quiet and none silent. Market carts began to clatter over the cobblestones long before dawn, and until well after midnight the human hive kept not only buzzing but chattering and shouting, and worst of all, building. Storeys were being piled up on the tops of houses and the hammering, shovelling, sawing and creaking went on from morning till night. To my amazement I did not fall into a rage over this turmoil. My nerves did not snap. On the contrary, I got a certain companionly comfort out of these varied human noises, almost a happiness in feeling no resentment toward my fellow bipeds for keeping up such a din. I was near enjoying it. In fact should have enjoyed it. Only the habit of getting into a fury over it prevented my doing so. Not for long! Since then I actually have enjoyed it because it has spelt the presence of fellow creatures.

Often it occurs to me to wonder what it would be like to find oneself in interstellar space, and what a desolation of loneliness would overtake one. So acute that one would welcome any living thing, even a monster come to devour one. The slum population of our cities is free from that fear. Is not that freedom worth the hygiene and even the comforts philanthropy tries to impose upon them!

A preoccupation with interstellar space, and measureless time as well, took hold of me after reading a good deal of popular astronomy and geology of a kind that a boy of thirteen or fourteen could grasp and enjoy. How much I understood I cannot remember, but I recall in what a turmoil of excitement it put my imagination. Quite subsided this turmoil never has, not even now. The contemplation of astronomic space and time easily puts me into a trance from which I wake not to actuality, but to vague cosmic visions. As a boy I used to revel in poems like Coleridge's *Hymn before Sunrise in the Vale of Chamonix,* Bryant's *Thanatopsis,* and verses, at that time even more impressive, by Derzhavin. Luckily I came just then across George Eliot's essay on Young's *Night Thoughts* and it pricked the cosmic bubble for me, leaving little but sentimentality behind.

I should confess that in those two or three years before I was fifteen I revelled in everything quantitative and statistical. I read with delight, as if it was a private happiness of my own, about the growth in population of the principal towns in the United States, about the advance in mileage of the railway system, about the accelerating speed of the same railways, about the days saved in crossing seas and oceans, about crop increase, etc., etc. In brief, at fourteen or fifteen, I passed through a stage of quantity worship. I soon outgrew it. It seems a phase through which young boys have to pass before puberty. I am not a little surprised to realize to what an extent this worship is carried on now by totalitarian regimes. Is the parallel thorough-going, or does it mean that these regimes are still in a pre-puberty stage?

The same volume or volumes of George Eliot's essays, in which I discovered the paper on Young's *Night Thoughts* that cured me of the cult of awe-inspiring stretches of time and space, were the first to present me with the idea that art values deserved as much consideration as those of life or of morals for shaping and directing actuality. Nothing I had yet encountered struck me as so startling, so improbable, so paradoxical even. How could such an absurdity be accepted by a boyish intellect as puritanical in outlook as mine. It stuck fast, however, like a seed sending out numberless roots and the problem has never since ceased to occupy me.

To return to my fellow creatures and my tolerance of ways previously found so annoying or even exasperating, a tolerance due to an affectionate acceptance of their wholeness, a jar of mixed pickles as it is, a very swill barrel even. I believe, I repeat, that if I live long enough I shall conquer my last indignation, my last despair, that over deliberate evil-doing. I shall be able to read Dickens and kindred writers who have a genius for presenting malignant characters; I shall not shrink from them as I have done hitherto—as from the sulphur and brimstone of hell.

5

Here another parenthesis suggested by the foregoing. It is about English humour. In wit, in French *esprit,* there is something censorious, and a satisfaction with being "holier than thou." Wit is apt to be at the expense of the subject, whether merely to humiliate him for fun, to chastise him for his good, or for both reasons together. To a great extent wit is optimistic, believing that by exercise of its function man can be improved.

Humour is not concerned with improving people. It accepts them as they are with their faults and foibles, chuckling over the one and putting up with the others, so long as these last do not too seriously interfere with the rights, the comforts and the safety of others. It arises from a gentle pessimism: the conviction that people are like that, and will not soon be otherwise, better make the best of it. Seeing that they can't change, why torment them and yourself by interfering, trying to shape them after your patterns, forcing them into your own moulds? Live and let live. Take them humorously. Be amused by what in them is quaint, absurd, ridiculous.

Does this attitude lead to the cult of liberty, the rights of the individual versus the state and even the community, the sacredness of the person? Or do these produce the attitude we recognize as humour? At all events they are interlaced and entwined.

Not all British people and their American offspring have these convictions about liberty. The militant puritans of old on both sides of the Atlantic can scarcely be credited with anything so human; nor can their contemporary descendants, the fanatical philanthropists, pacifists, and lightning world-improvers. They can be as little credited with a sense of humour as with a feeling for liberty. If there have been puritan humourists, their humour must have been grim.

6

Returning to the subject in hand, my faith in humanity: having got the better of most of my annoyances, disapprovals, exasperations, and despairs over it, having lived and read and thought about it and discussed it for many years, I am now convinced that this faith is justified by what man has achieved already in the relatively short time that he has been human. Think of his origins. A mere animal among the animals, neither as strong, nor as swift, nor as beautiful as many of his fellow-animals. In the course of a few hundred thousand years he has risen as much above mere animality as his proud cathedrals and palaces, his comfortable dwellings and his lofty towers known as skyscrapers rise above the rock shelters and leaf huts that were his primitive dwellings. Indeed, at times I compare our race to a structure of many storeys. The more humanized we get the more storeys has our House of Life. At the bottom live those who rise little above other domesticated animals. It is well with them and they should be properly fed, kept clean and healthy in body and mind, and treated as the androplasm out of which will spring more humanized men and women. These progressively occupy the mounting storeys to the top, where abide the few who come nearest to a humanly conceivable perfection.

Each of us is in himself like such a building. In the lower storeys we live with our animal needs, animal greeds, and animal passions. Woe if we neglect the first, ignore the second, and pretend to be free from the last! No matter how high we rise we must never lose sight, never cease being aware, of the animal basis of our nature. If we do, we lose the sense of things. We get vapid, vague, hypocritical, arrogant, insolent. The tall structure that we have become turns into a tower of Babel, toppling over and confounding its builder. The stars in their courses fight against *hybris* and never fail to down it. And *hybris* is due largely, although not wholly, to ignoring human nature whether on its animal or spiritual side, as the so-called optimistic idealists—their variety is legion—do with the one, and the pessimistic authoritarian totalitarians with the other.

I am carried along by this faith in human destiny as Sir Christopher Wren, had he been allowed to rebuild London after the Great Fire; or Ledoux, at the dawn of the industrial age, had he been able to realize his plan for a noble manufacturing town. They could not expect to see their vision materialize in their lifetime, but that certainty would not have cooled their ardour, diminished their zeal, or enfeebled their faith.

So with us. Prophets and poets and artists in their consciously creative way, and in their wake men of action unconsciously executing what the first designed, have contributed toward the building of the City of Man, as do the men and women who try to live up to a standard that does not substitute comfort for happiness, as do those who take life as an apprenticeship, as an education. Blessed are they who are aware of this, and if many insist on designating this ideal as the City of God, let them. The Gospels make little if any distinctions between the Son of Man and the Son of God!

7

Now for my faith in IT. "From hope and fear set free"—not quite, yet enough to be liberated from preoccupying cares for the future, a distant future at any rate. For the near, the nearest future, I still have anxieties but only because I am living in a country to which I am so attached that I cannot abandon it, although it is as good as at war with my own. If conditions were normal I should be as little troubled by fear as transported by hope. I should take every day, and every waking hour, as if we were no longer filled with expectation but entirely given over to realization. Even as it is I could say to most moments as they pass, *Verbleibe doch, Du bist so schön,* except that, beautiful as they are, I do not ask them to linger. I know they will be followed by others as beautiful.

IT is every experience that is ultimate, valued for its own sake and, in our own intention, intransitive, although it affects others and ourselves as well to the extent that we remain under the horizon of the moment—I mean under the threshold of awareness. IT is aesthetical and, to the largest extent that the two can be kept separated, not ethical. IT accepts what is as if what is were a work of art in which the qualities so outweighed the faults that these could be ignored. IT is incapable of analysis, requires no explanations and no apology, is self-evident and right. One may sing about it but not discuss it. IT is the most immediate and mystical way.

In childhood and youth one had many moments of contact with IT but did not recognize them. In my case, it is true, I was conscious of these moments when I was passing into manhood. I delighted in knowing as well as feeling that I was young, with life spreading before me as a landscape under a golden haze half revealing objects too fascinating to approach, too alluring to keep away from. I knew that youth was IT, but what at the time I did not know was that this ITness was made up of a subject and an object. The subject was the psychophysiological sentience which revelled in an ecstasy of physical well-being. This euphoric condition radiated into time, into the future, lighting up the object, a vast expanse crowded with possibilities of adventurous happiness. What at the same period of existence I did not suspect was that these promises were not promises of happiness to come but realizations produced by the tingle of the blood in my veins and the glow in my viscera. I did not know that these promises were but the exhilarations of the forces then favouring me. The promise in happiness was the language of my then present happiness. For contemplation of the future, as distinct from precise planning for it is, I repeat, but an adjective on that substantive, the present. And seeing that youth while it is present is almost universally the moment of highest well-being, it is natural enough that later on we should look backward with yearning to the time when we were looking forward.

So I knew that being young was IT, and felt no eagerness to get through with it, and to plunge into a career that would bring at once independence, responsibility and power. I had little lust for power and no desire for responsibility, but an invincible passion for independence. It was no easy matter to attain it; and much time and energy were wasted. But I have attained it. Not many have gone through life with so few restrictions to their freedom of action, freedom of contact and, need one add, freedom of thought. Not many are the hours of labour I have done out of compulsion. Even the work that brought in money has almost never been of a kind I should not have done in the course of study and research. I have no doubt said this more than once already. It is my chief pride, and I cannot help boasting of it.

Until thirty or so I was young enough to live in a magical universe, a universe full of glamour through which I saw what was for the time being conventionally regarded as the actual world, as if through a prism. And till then almost everything that meant anything was IT. Then something happened. I was pushed out of Eden and found myself in a realm where men and women did not live for IT but were invariably doing something for the sake of something else. True, the most fortunate did it with gusto, with the satisfaction of healthy exercise of function. They were, however, so preoccupied with the next that they found no time to feel how much they were enjoying the passing moment. Who in a society crush has not encountered the "going-on" look in faces searching for the person they would more profitably be with than with yourself! And except for the alcove, all life seemed to be lived for a moment beyond and never for the present one. "Jam yesterday and jam to-morrow, but never jam to-day."

I could not resist the contagion, although often enough, and at the most inopportune moments, I would get a sudden chill at my heart and say, "This is not IT." For some thirty years—as many again as my whole previous existence—I wandered through this wilderness encountering now and again refreshing oases, but seldom giving myself up with complete abandon to any person, idea or thing. Part of me was not there, but already elsewhere.

At last the indifference and selectiveness due to the wisdom of experience, and in even greater measure to instinctive economizing of diminished energies, began to turn me back to my essential realities; and by the time I was seventy, all ambition spent and passion whether of sense, heart or mind stilled, I could return to my long interrupted ITness. Not merely to take it up where I had left it but with an awareness, an understanding, a wonder, a gratitude, a joy that one could not have experienced young when one took as a matter of course what one found at hand when roused to consciousness. Is not life genuinely lived a long and roundabout pilgrimage back to the sources of our being and the rudiments of our universe, to which we return with an appreciation, a comprehension, a penetration that could not have been felt at the start? Thus for each of us there are the tears and the joy of the Prodigal's return, and the fatted calf, in the sense that life is IT whatever it brings.

Ambition spent, literally, I have no desire for fame and fortune beyond what I enjoy already. I am without the wish to be remembered, and avoid doing the little one might do decently to prolong one's memory a while. I should not mind even if I were clean forgotten before my mortal end by all but intimates. I believe that I have worked for my passage from eternity to eternity, and have not been a mere parasite on the ocean of time. That is satisfaction and comfort enough.

As for passion, I still crave for affection, and enjoy intelligent appreciation of my company. Sensual passion is no longer concentrated upon one or two persons, but has been diffused. So diffused that I could caress any living thing that was not unpleasant. All young people of either sex, and women past the canonical age. I am aware that old men like to fondle young women. I know also that in Paris there are morbid males called *frôleurs,* subject to police correction. I trust that I shall be able to avoid the senility of the first and the distress of the other. Nor does it escape me that lovely creatures offer their cheeks to kiss because they rank me with fathers and even grandfathers, not with their lovers. I seldom want it otherwise. An unceasing affection possesses me for all that is, and all that is not ugly, nor vulgar, nor evil. Nor do I mean evil in a moral sense only. For me it includes ugliness and vulgarity as well, despite the fact that both these terms have lost almost all ethical meaning and connote aesthetic values chiefly. I could caress not only men and women and children and the animals that would submit to it, but trees as well. Trees perhaps most of all. Long before I felt so indulgent and kindly to members of my own species I used to think that if I loved human beings as I loved trees I should be a saint. To this day the death of a noble cypress or mighty oak or tremulous poplar affects me more than that of all but few men and women whose necrology I read in the newspapers.

A little while ago I mentioned getting the better of a dislike for babies and little ones. I used to associate them with the confusion, the noise, the lack of intelligence that not only got on my nerves but made me doubt of the universe. The conversion was completed by the happy accident of a child of only four in the house, so lovely to look at, so playful, so merry, so gay that it was an animal joy, as well as an aesthetic delight, to have him around. I suddenly realized what heaven-sent playthings such babies might be, and how not only mothers but even fathers craved to have one on hand, with new ones coming on as the first were growing too old. And how grandparents and even great-grandparents revelled in them more and more as their own age increased.

My belief is that when we ripen for an experience it is some work of art, visual, verbal or musical that reveals its full sense and helps us to its utmost enjoyment. I was beginning to caress with my eye the lovely nude of my wife's infant great-grandson and to delight in his gambols, his whirling, his dancing when I left for a journey to Dalmatia. On a radiant July morning a motor-boat sped me from Spalato to Traù, and I devoted the entire day to the Romanesque churches and Venetian palaces and loggias of that noble and exquisite town. I returned the next day with voracity and leisure to "loaf and feast my soul." So I went back to the cathedral Baptistery and became aware of what my eyes must have seen time and again but had never taken in, a rout of naked babies in relief, more vital, more merry, more ecstatically happy than even Luca della Robbia's, and Donatello's in Florence. They communicated their joy to me, and in the midst of it I felt that the little great-grandson could hold his own with any of them.

8

"Laisser tout cela!" moaned the dying Mazarin, taking a last look at his art treasures and his books. I could leave mine (if one may venture to compare so small with so great) without a pang, if I could hope that the books I have so carefully selected and accumulated in the last fifty years would remain together, shelved and catalogued as they now are. I understand the vanity of such a wish and how mummy-like, after a while, the realization would be. Yes, but for two or three generations it might retain a kind of life if in matters of scholarship it was kept up to date. For more than a couple of generations it would be difficult to keep the character that a private person gives to books collected to inform, enlighten and entertain himself and his kind. After that it must be institutionalized or cease to be.

That is the last and only attachment to a personal future from which I have not yet emancipated myself. I hope to live long enough to get rid of even that relict of the vanity of vanities. Not that I could not enjoy the idea that the house, the garden, the

works of art, and above all, the books gathered in a lifetime should continue indefinitely to serve and delight future generations; but I want to contemplate it as a thing of beauty in nature or in art that one does not dream of possessing, not as something attached to my own ego. In fact, I could wish to be as free from the desire to perpetuate my accumulations as were the Goncourts. They sent everything to the hammer so that others might enjoy a like pleasure with what they had in acquiring each item one by one.

I must confess to another vanity with regard to the future. It is the eagerness to know what the next day will bring forth. I became aware of it when, fifty-three years ago, happening to be in Rome with William James, he told me one afternoon that he had just seen F. U. H. Myers die, and that the last thing the dying man asked for was the morning paper. Yes, I too would wish to live to the following day, so as to see what was happening before I left this realm of being. And that desire has grown with age. At present I want to live to see the end of the war, I want it very much. Foolish boy, don't you recall that Armistice Day 1918 was one of the most distressing you ever passed. You had such a clear Pisgah sight of how the peace would turn out. It turned out no better than your fears. Why expect anything better from human nature when this war is over? We plant hope on our graves, as Schiller tells us. To be perfectly truthful I should add that if the war turns out as I hope, I should want to enjoy saying, "I told you so." Yet, I know that I should not do it, when it came to the point.

So, on the whole, the future does not trouble me much, and the past scarcely at all. Would one change any part of one's past if one could? Would one begin by having another father and mother? Each particular event would not affect one's individuality so much as having other parents. Cumulatively, they alter and transform us as much. Either result would be at the expense of our present self, our conscious personality, our familiar stream of consciousness. Are we ready to sacrifice it in exchange for another ego? I cannot even conceive of such a thing, although again and again we have wished it, little calculating the costs. I go so far as to doubt whether we truly want undone anything that has happened to us, no matter how recently, not to speak of long ago. We may regret that it was so; but, being so, we cannot with a whole mind wish it otherwise.

Having nearly emancipated myself from the future and entirely from the past, I am ready to live in the present, and to enjoy the exercise of the functions that use and wont have left unimpaired to work smoothly, and with a pleasant output of energy.

One habit I have not yet succeeded in getting rid of: the inveterate one of feeling that when at home I must sit at my desk for so long each day to write, not letters whether of business or of friendship, but printable stuff, even when there is no idea of publishing connected with it. If I have failed to do it, I feel morally hangdoggy and physically unclean.

I sit down with plenty to say that the morning hours have flashed into my half-waked, passive mind. I know so well what I want to say that it is a disgrace as well as a torment to be so baffled the moment I try to put pen to paper. All at once words have deserted me, ink has dried up, my thoughts were mocking me. I had better give up. I persist, and scribble as listlessly as, in idle and bored moods, one scratches lines on paper or digs diagrams with a stick in the sand. Although to my amazement this scribble does make sense, it seldom gives satisfaction. In short, I know too well what, in all its varieties, good writing should be and often is, to place myself among those who practice it.

I go on blaming myself for having failed to master a vocabulary and a phraseology and a rhythm, that in short I have not acquired a style of writing which would enable me to tell others, thereby increasing my own pleasure, what I now see and feel about the microcosm—in the literal sense—to which my microcosm is now reduced.

It is distressing to be so invincibly ignorant of the names of flowers and of plants in general, to have so few epithets for colours. True, I share the last failing with most people, but real writers get around it in ways more hidden and insinuating than the crude comparison with minerals and vegetables. Strange how little in this respect we have advanced on Homer, who used the same word for blue and green although he surely must have perceived the difference! What victims we are of our inglorious muteness, and when we do speak how aphasic we are apt to be! The most gifted authors can seldom say anything satisfactory about a concrete object without singing it; I wish I could sing about flowers and colours. Each day I seem to appreciate both more. I look and say: "What have my eyes been that I have not realized as I do this morning the spread of that rose, the turn of its petals, the exact shade of its varying reds or yellows or whites; or the translucency of the tissues in the rhododendron, azalea or morning-glory."

And as for the colours!

Colour is something that has been revealed to me, has grown upon me with the years. I was not born with a feeling for it, and in Boston sixty-five years ago there was little to generate and educate the sense of it. Of course I enjoyed it as the garment of the shapes I saw, but not sensually for its own sake.

One summer morning tens of years later I wound my way up the staircase leading from the lower to the upper church of Saint Francis of Assisi. I stepped suddenly into the nave and found myself immersed in an atmosphere of disembodied colour. It did not belong to any shape. It was in the air, produced by reflections, from the stained glass, the frescoed walls and ceiling. I neither saw nor felt either. I was bathed in colour. I breathed it. It was a revelation almost as rejuvenating as the one I had years before with regard to form and movement while facing the façade of San Pietro at Spoleto.

I say rejuvenating, because I felt as if born to a new kingdom, to an enlarged life. Since then I have got to enjoy colour as much as smell, almost as much as taste, and as sensuously.

9

So for the years, the months, the weeks, perhaps the days only that I am still to live, I am living IT. I am well aware how precarious, how fragile it is. Since childhood I have seldom said good-bye to persons I was attached to without asking myself whether I should ever see them again—even if the separation was to be one only of hours. Later I became aware that this was a sybaritic attitude, in the sense that it enhanced the passing moment with ideated anticipations of longing, yearning, and sweet regret, thereby adding to the pleasure of seeing again the person one feared, faintly, almost playfully, yet did fear, one might never see again. Likewise with places, with landscapes. If I returned to them I might find them changed, as so many have since I first knew them. Brick-kilns lead up to romantic towns perched high in the Abruzzi; the nobly classical waterfalls of Terni have been sucked up in the obscenities of steel and ironworks; sugar factories blacken with smoke the Nile beyond Luxor; jam cookeries disfigure Brussa; insolent hotels bar the entrance to Assisi. Constant change, and even if for the better, is rarely welcome because of one's affection for the past! I would therefore want to extract all I could from the passing moment, as if something would be irretrievably lost if I did not gather it into my memory. There it remains safe while I live. If only I could communicate it to others, then I should sing *Nunc dimittis.* Which brings me back to the regret that I have not acquired the technique and style of a *Dichter*—of one who, with words, can make others feel what he felt.

I wonder, though, whether there ever lived an artist, great or humble, but artist enough to attempt to grasp, to shape, to present any particle of chaos, who on completing a task felt that it adequately expressed what he had seen, what he had been penetrated with throughout, and wanted to re-create.

IT, again, means taking things as they come, as one did as a young person when one felt no responsibility for them but took them as a matter of course. The difference is, again, that instead of taking things thoughtlessly and with scant appreciation one now receives them with grateful recognition of what they offer and an almost holy joy in their being. IT comes to mean taking life ritually as something holy, of mystical import and in one's thought ideatedly—if not in realizable actuality as a sacred performance. From childhood up I have had the dream of a life lived as a sacrament. With the years it merged into the wish that it could be lived with the significance of a work of art: not imitating any visual, musical or literary masterpieces but an art as independent, as autonomous, as each of the arts should be and like them flowing from the same source in the human spirit.

The genius who revealed to me what from childhood I had been instinctively tending toward was Walter Pater in his *Marius,* his *Imaginary Portraits,* his *Child in the House,* his *Emerald Uthwart,* his *Demeter.* It is for that I have loved him since youth and shall be grateful to him even to the House of Hades where, in the words of Nausicaa to Odysseus, I shall hail him as god. It was he who encouraged me to extract from the chaotic succession of events in the common day what was wholesome and sweet, what fed and sustained the spirit, what could soar and take Pisgah sights of promised lands and yet be happy to return to the "kindred points of heaven and home."

"Home"—what is it? Is it the place where one was born, where one's forbears were born and died, where one spent one's earliest years? Few in America, even if native, can claim such a privilege; still less those who were brought there with other memories already filling their heads. As these memories grow dimmer with the years, as relations left behind die or cease to exist for one, the notion of home is banished for a time. It is only when I left Boston after graduating at Harvard that I realized how much home-feeling I attached to that to me so hospitable, so human, so highly civilized city. And ever since, after fifty-five years, it remains "home," although it knows me not and perhaps would not claim me if it did.

Home for me has acquired yet another sense. Not of a place but of a household, and therein first and foremost the persons composing it. Of them, as I am not writing memoirs, I shall not speak; but of the house gladly.

What is a house? Is it, as Corbusier with fanatical fervour urges, a living machine, approaching as much as possible to an up-to-date clinic with the furniture suggesting and almost smelling of the operating-room? A living machine it was, no doubt, to our paleolithic ancestors, a strictly totalitarian affair, although phenic acid was in the remote future. They discovered it ready-made in caves and half-made in rock shelters; or they constructed roughly roofed windscreens out of reeds and mats. Later, from the bronze age onwards, a house began to take on something of the cosiness of a cottage, beyond the mere requirements of a living-machine. By the eighteenth century, with Georgian in England and *Louis Quinze* in France, for those who could afford it, it became, inside and out, a paradise.

A house can be still another thing: part of one's raiment, the outermost garment, the one manifested to the largest public by which the world that knows one least will think it knows one best. It has therefore a social and even political importance beyond one's clothes even, for these are seen by fewer people: acquaintances, friends who can penetrate under one's outer garments and some one or two who get so far as to see one naked and unashamed.

I cannot penetrate a house for the first time without imagining what sort of person could have exhaled it, by living there. Then I wonder what it would be like to occupy it myself, and what would happen to me if I did, what one would become and how one would end. I surely would end, after no matter what palaces and pleasures, with a longing for a home *parva sed apta mihi*—small but "my size," as Ariosto engraved over his unpalatian abode in palatian Ferrara. A ready-made house is like ready-made clothes. There are average men and women whom ready-made apparel of the smartish and fetching kinds suits as well as if the best tailors and dressmakers in London and Paris had lovingly worked for them. Blessed are these average, even high average, men and women. Those of us who are not "standard size" never look ourselves in such clothes. And besides they challenge our intimate sense of uniqueness to which those who have it cling for dear life.

I remember on my first return to New York after an absence of seven years in Europe, walking up Fifth Avenue from Forty-second Street toward Central Park, passing Loire châteaux cheek by jowl with Florentine palaces and wanting to plant before the grand entrance of each a cast-iron interrogation point high enough to top the roof. Likewise with the inside of these same edifices. François I, Henri II, Tuscan, Venetian—what had they to do with the people who paid for them and pretended to live in them? Could they ever feel that they belonged there? I recall one in particular. The entrance hall was a Quattrocento Florentine cloister and it led to a Moorish patio, both as genuine as possible—under the circumstances. The patio was furnished as a parlour of the most opulent kind and from it one was led into a room glazed with sombre mediaeval glass, hung with dark wine-coloured cut velvet and lit by funeral wax candles. The walls were studded with bronze processional crosses dating from the eleventh and twelfth centuries. Penitential chill prevailed. I was told by the hosts, who were doing the honours, that this was where they dined. Who would have guessed it? Thence we were taken from hall to hall, each crowded with priceless works of art attached to the walls, placed invitingly on stands, proudly erect on pedestals, so that one had to brush gingerly between them. I kept looking at these splendours while casting an occasional side glance at the lord and lady of the domain, wondering what connection there was between these two, surely not to the manner born, and all this plunder. Was it possible that they actually lived there, and that in this palace there was not hidden away a cosy little room or two where they could feel at home? Apparently not, for the hostess took us with pride to a bathroom that the Agrippinas and Faustinas of imperial Rome could not have dreamt of and drew particular attention to the fact that the taps were of gold. The visit ended with an exhibition of the clothespress for endless raiments and of a cunningly lit depository for innumerable pairs of shoes and slippers. And that was perhaps the part of this Aladdin's wonder that seemed the least unreal in any human sense. Real, too, in the most up-to-date use of the word, were the litter and rubbish that filled the sunk area lining this treasure-house.

My house, I trust, does express my needs, my tastes and aspirations. It is a library with living-rooms attached. These are both spacious and comfortable yet with a touch of old Italian severity that might depress the happy victims of our "interior decorators." One of these, and not the meanest, came on her honeymoon, and told me frankly that the house was cheerless, that it gave no sign of taste, that the furniture lacked elegance and finish, was in fact rough and ready. I humbly submitted that I had thought of none of these things but only of an interior that suited my muscular and respiratory ideations with regard to space and my eyes with regard to shapes and colours. The pieces of furniture are of a size suitable to that purpose and so is the rest, the hangings, the paintings, the few art objects.

Let me add parenthetically that these hangings, paintings, these art objects were not acquired first and foremost with an eye to making a collection, but almost exclusively to adorn my abode. When that was completed some thirty years ago I stopped buying. Indeed I have always disclaimed being a collector. Such a one loves to compete, to get the better of the seller, to gloat over the object as a scalp or trophy, and finally either to enshrine it in his halo of self-satisfaction or to sell it at a high profit in money or pride.

I had no such thought, and indeed in the course of forty or fifty years I have not—to use the hallowed phrase of collectors— "parted with" half a dozen inferior objects. As for buying for a rise, I could have made a fortune acquiring Cézannes at a time when they could be had for "a few coppers," when indeed a friend of that time, Egisto Fabbri, bought a dozen or more to sell them several decades later for many millions of francs. I could not see myself living with masterpieces so little in harmony with an Italian dwelling. When the house was at long last furnished and the works of art in their place, it did not occur to me that I was in possession of more than could be gathered by any student taking advantage of his acquired knowledge and exercised taste. It took the scattering of most private collections all over Europe to make me realize that mine was one of the best remaining.

I require many fittings from my tailor. Not that I as much as think of looking elegant, or of wishing to be smart or dressy in my clothes. I want to feel and look myself. They never suit me till I have lived myself into them. That done I cling to them for dear life. So it was, so it is, with my house. Although I had so gifted an architect as Cecil Pinsent, who often understood my wants better than I did, it half killed me to get it into shape, and it was not when I gave up the struggle. With the years I got used to it, stopped seeing blemishes or defects, stopped bothering about fading, damage, moths, decay, and now after many years I love it as much as one can love any object or complex of objects not human. It is a *machine à vivre,* if you like, as there is a similar machine in our bodies, but like my body my house has a soul—I hope.

10

I have a garden too, as I mentioned earlier. Unless it pours with rain I run through it at least once a day, to taste the air, to listen to the sound of birds and streams, to admire the flowers and trees.

I wonder whether art has a higher function than to make us feel, appreciate and enjoy natural objects for their art value? So, as I walk in the garden, I look at the flowers and shrubs and trees and discover in them an exquisiteness of contour, a vitality of edge or a vigour of spring as well as an infinite variety of colour that no artifact I have seen in the last sixty years can rival. And beyond the garden, as I walk on the olive-crowned, pine-plumed, cypress-guarded hills, I enjoy the effect of clouds under the high and spacious dome of the sky, the hazes between me and the horizon toward Siena, toward Volterra, toward Pisa, toward Carrara—hazes leaden on dull days, silvery in the winter, pearly in spring and autumn, and golden at midsummer. Each day, as I look, I wonder where my eyes were yesterday. Why did I not perceive the beauty of that lichen-trimmed tree-trunk as gorgeous as an Aztec or Maya mosaic; of that moss of a soft emerald that beds your eye as reposefully as the greens in a

Giorgione or Bonifazio; and why had I been blind to the jewelled elaboration of the honey-suckle and to the enamelled elegance of the purplish-black and ruby butterfly that flutters about those slopes? So, health permitting as happily as it still does, I do not need to roam nor even to soar; for every morning, every afternoon as I go out of doors, I discover more than enough newness to suffice for the day. I should still love real wandering, journeying where there are no inns, no railways, and scarcely roads. I should love to re-visit all the scenery I have enjoyed in the last fifty years and more. Yet I do not hanker for it inordinately. I do not even have to look at pictures, for I have become my own painter and can see "in nature" more beauty than they can reveal to me in their compositions. I require no sculpture, because my imagination has become so moulding that, having about me such models as the Tuscan peasantry, I can visualize them as statues in movement.

When I do look at works of art, if they are works of art and not objects of novelty and curiosity only—in other words, when they are master-pieces—I am apt to see in them, as in natural objects, some aspect, whether of shape or colour or quality, that I never perceived before. Thus far I have exhausted nothing that the human spirit has created. I can still enjoy Gray's *Elegy;* I can still live in the world of Grimm's or Andersen's fairy tales or of the *Arabian Nights* with the same unquestioning trust in their reality—

their own realm of reality—as I did when, as a lad, I read them for the first time. Nor have the myths of the Greeks, the Hebrews and the Northmen lost their fascination. Needless to add that the classics in the few languages accessible to me keep their timeless vitality and unhushed appeal. Unfortunately, reading a book consumes hours and hours of leisure, or I should be reperusing the ever-contemporary ones every little while. There, by the way, pictures and other visual objects enjoy a great advantage; for one can muster hundreds and even thousands, adequately reproduced, in the time it takes to read one considerable volume. There again, as I may have already discussed at length here or elsewhere, lies the chief handicap to the criticism of literature. I can glance at a hundred works of art in a few minutes, taste, appreciate, rank and classify them while they are there before my eyes. In literature, an art which, like music, has the passing of time for its canvas, but takes much more time for its enjoyment, understanding, appreciation, comparison, judgement must rely on memory and is inevitably its victim. Well may it be questioned, therefore, whether satisfactory criticism of literature is in the nature of the case possible.

When young I too in the field of the spirit was a food gatherer, a huntsman, a nomad, with their incapacity for intensive exploitation, or their need of keeping ever on the move to fresh fields and pastures new. Now, while I still enjoy the fruit of the familiar as well as the unexpected and exotic, I have no conscious need of change, no itch for newness. I like to eat the same food every day, having that alone in common with Napoleon, who could eat a fowl at every meal. I like to live in the same place. I zestfully do the same things. The more I do a thing, the more I want to do it. And so with friends. I prefer old ones to new ones and do not tire of them. Of course old friends are less exciting, less stimulating. We have explored them to the extent that we can, for there is a limit beyond which it is not given to the most intimate companions to penetrate and understand each other. The crowning happiness of friendship is when one loves just to be with the friend and feels no need to speak. Being in the same room, breathing the same air, thinking perhaps of the same range of things are pleasure enough. Edith Wharton, after evenings so spent, would say, "What a heavenly time we have had!" And so with walking. Often enough it is over trails where one has to go Indian file. Talk would be difficult, yet it makes all the difference whether I have a real companion or not.

11

But to return to my house: if I am not deprived of the use of it through the absurdities of politics and am free to finish my days in my garden and adjacent countryside, I shall enjoy the realization of what the training of a lifetime, a long lifetime, has fitted me for. Every experience still awaiting me, great or small, will be a work of art, an ultimate, will be IT; but at the same time, like a work of art, again operative as example, as suggestion, perhaps even as starting point for others.

Earlier I boasted of having conquered hurry. I wish I could conquer greed. I do not refer to food or drink or lust, for I am temperate with regard to animal appetites. I wish I could get the better of the hunger and thirst for information that possesses me always, and most of all when I glance at shelf after shelf of books treating of the manifold matters that mark the steps of mankind's humanization from Peking and Piltdown and Neanderthal skulls to the man of the present moment. Whatever throws light on this subject I am as eager to read as the stories of Robin Hood, Rinaldo Rinaldini or Ragged Dick when I was a small boy. I read or am read to half the day, but it would take days that were as long as weeks to get in all I want to read at any moment.

Likewise with writing. It remains a torment, a gentle one but yet a torment. I still feel that I must get rid of so much ink every day. At bottom it is a physical matter, not more praiseworthy than habit. In consciousness, however, it takes the aspect of a self-disapproval to be avoided.

When much younger I had an old friend, a spoiled child of fortune, living opulently high over Naples on the rents that a big town in New York State tributed to him. He used to say that to live comfortably one had to have a little more money and a little less time than one could use. I have had no experience enabling me to judge how it would feel to have more money than one knew what to do with. With regard to time, I can give full adherence to the Civil War veteran's adage. Truly, as I walk through my house I can only say in words taken and twisted from the sententious poet of more than one century ago that: "Every prospect pleases and nothing is vile."

My library contains nearly everything, although not everything that my lust for knowledge requires. It is rare that I cannot lay hands on a publication referred to in whatever volume I happen to be reading. For fifty years and more I have been gathering books for the time when I should have leisure. I have never bought a book for its rarity from a collector's point of view. I was not aware of possessing an all but *unicum* in the shape of a sixteenth-century pamphlet regarding Michelangelo that my friend Ernst Steinmann discovered on my shelves—the Steinmann who not only was one of the most fruitful workers in the Renaissance field but the spiritual founder and first director of the Anglo-German-Jewish institution for liberal learning called the Hertziana, at present serving Nazi propaganda rather than culture of any kind. My books are books for use, tools, not works of art, although I take more pleasure in reading *Dichtung*—poetry, whether in verse or prose—in shapely type on a well-set page of hand-made paper, crisp, elastic, almost musical as you turn a leaf. I certainly enjoy the Bible, Saint Augustine, Dante, Shakespeare, Boccaccio, Wordsworth, Goethe, Keats, Shelley, etc., etc., much more in the Doves, the Ashendene, the Bremen presses than I do in ordinary editions. But nothing would induce me to read a seventeenth-century author in the wretched print of that period, certainly not Shakespeare in the first and the following folio—as distressing to the eye as to the understanding. And yet America takes pride in a citizen whose wealth and lack of imagination enabled him to accumulate twenty copies of the first folio. With what object, one may ask, except the sadistic one of preventing nineteen other libraries from deriving what little philological profit or associative sentimentality their possession can still yield?

For me the main object is to have books at hand so as to be able to use them when one is piping hot with eagerness for them and malleably receptive to what one can get out of them. If survival after death were conceivable, I should wish to be the indwelling soul of my house and library. To speak more grossly, I should like to haunt it, and use it the way the archangels did in one of Anatole France's stories.

So after a fashion I have attained Goethe's promise that what one ardently desires when young one will realize in old age. I am not far from my nirvana, I am in sight of IT.

And IT is a feeling of oneness with the landscape, with the house, and all that therein is, with the folk that pass, with the people one frequents, with one's occupation whether mental or manual, a oneness so complete that it knows nothing outside itself. In other words IT is a mystic union.

CASA AL DONO, VALLOMBROSA.
July 25, 1941

EPILOGUE

I finished writing these glimpses into myself when Italy was already at war with the Western Powers. Since then, there have intervened four years of a war so discouraging to hopes for humanizing mankind that one might be tempted to ask the Creator to throw up the experiment—as many an inventor and artist has done in this time.

And yet I have come through it spiritually unharmed and physically undamaged, although aged and enfeebled.

To my surprise I turned out to have a confidence in my own pattern of things that nothing could shake, not even Dunkirk and the so-perilous subsequent months. By October '40 every qualm had left me. The British could hold their own till we Americans came in; and that we should

I never doubted. Not that it would be in good time. Once in, the war could not end but with the crushing of Nazism. It never occurred to me that America could lose a war and a similar "animal faith"—to use Santayana's phrase—kept away fear that serious harm might happen to me.

But this war, the most destructive, surely, and perhaps the cruellest in history, has it affected my outlook, my feelings about the value of life, and my hopes for the future of mankind?

Not essentially. I have never ignored the evil that still lurks in the hell that each of us carries in his heart; what a struggle it was to keep it down; what the consequences might be of letting it loose. Song and story, fable and chronicle, have taught us that mankind has not only Olympus but Tartarus in its breast, not only Walhall but Nifelheim. History is, or should be, the account of the struggle between the forces of good and evil. If the last chapter seems the most terrifying of all, nor ended quite with the defeat of Germany and Japan, it is owing not only to the magnifying and distorting perspective of being too near to events and being overwhelmed by detail, but also to the fact that never before our machine age could a people running amok have had the means, the instruments wherewith to be as destructive and bestial as it can be now.

In other fields beside the mechanical, it may not be worse. We know that in our countries, including Italy, the war has made us think deeper and more clearly about the evils of nationalism

—and how to cure them. I am encouraged rather than disheartened by the fact that we are eschewing perfectionism and have concluded humbly to build the new storeys to the House of Life on massive walls, resting firmly on sound foundations rather than in Cloudcuckootown. A riddance of verbiage is the beginning of international wisdom. Edifices put up quietly, inch by inch, are less likely to be too weak to resist attack and abler to support what burden the future may pile upon them.

In truth, I believe, we are more aware than ever before of the dangers threatening us and more eager to obviate them. Indeed we seem rather to wallow in the prospect of trouble. Thus I do not believe that in the present historical horizon Germany can again become a serious menace to our peace. Certainly not if we treat her fearlessly, intelligently and humanely, avoiding some of the ways pursued by us between the two wars.

We must not attempt to bottle up her gifts, her energies, her constructive and productive qualities. Above all we must not humiliate her. We should avoid doing anything that we cannot justify morally by neutral standards. Let us not imitate the Nazis in racialism to begin with and then in writing down the entire German race as beasts beyond the pale of humanity. How absurd and wicked this is we Americans should know well, seeing what an extraordinary percentage of our high command in both army and navy bear German names. Nor are the same kind of names absent from civilian services. They are, with rarest exceptions, sons or grandsons of immigrants from the Fatherland. What does that mean but that if you transplant the German to our spiritual soil he turns out the best of Americans?

The loss of individuals in the flower of their years has been, at least in Germany and Russia, unprecedented, and it is to be feared that we shall be made aware of it in the near future, by the rarity of gift among the people who carry on each nation's business in whatever field. The more the pity, as we shall have greater need than ever of brain and brawn.

We shall muddle through. I say "muddle" deliberately; for I believe the problems facing us are too numerous, too complicated, and too interlocked to be treated by any now existing intelligence, although we must encourage what intelligence there is to do its utmost.

Put our situation at its worst. Paint it as black as you can, make it as hopeless. Yet mankind has been through as bad. "As bad!" Surely we are much better off than Mycenaeans after the Doric invasion, or the Latin world after the crumbling away of the Western Empire. Both recovered: Greece to become the model for all modes of thought and feeling, expression and action; and our Western world to form, after centuries, the mediæval civilization, with its previously unimaginable achievements in social organization, in philosophy, in the visual arts and in architecture particularly. Should we sink, as we may, even lower than we have already, yet we have not lost nor are we likely to lose our science, our mechanical knowledge and inventiveness, or our accumulated information on all subjects or the masterpieces of our literature and our arts. Happily, nothing has been wholly lost that is essential to continuation of either our material or our immaterial civilization. Only our artisanship has suffered in a way from which it may take generations to recover.

I am well aware that I am speaking of myself who, in a long life devoted to historical thinking, has been taught to take wide perspectives and give time its due. In the course of history what are a few generations or even centuries, if one is sure that a long period of high civilization is to follow! To follow, to last! Perhaps it is in our descendants' hands to make it last for ever, constantly improving and advancing until mankind is completely humanized.

There are, no doubt, possibilities of complete disaster. One is the decay of stock. Against this, it may be affirmed that despite the chatter about degeneracy, decline, decadence, the white man has perhaps never been so healthy, so "fit" as in our time. The danger at present is the other way: that he will burst with energy.

The other possibility is that, indifferent to results as we are when it is a question of exercising functions that imperatively insist on being exercised, physicists and chemists in the course of experimenting may destroy mankind, if not all life and the planet itself.

Such a prospect is too remote to disturb me, or to embitter my last years.

The Hindu at forty was commanded by his religion to retire from the world, to become a bhikshu, and to spend the rest of his days in trying to find his soul. I have reached twice that age and at times am put out with myself for still wanting to produce, to publish; instead of abandoning myself to the ecstatic union with nature and with art for which eighty years of conditioning, of training, of education have fitted me. How often, as I stroll in the garden or take longer walks or as I glance at books in my library or think of the sights and sounds to which I still can find access, do I chide myself for letting the itch for transitive activities control me.

I am so fitted now to take in, to appreciate, to worship not only beauty in nature and in art, but the beauty of holiness (to which I have always been sensitive) and of that most wonderful of all masterpieces, a man or woman morally, intellectually, and physically satisfactory. Even the full possession of one of these qualities, provided it does not reject the others, enshrines the individual in a halo of wholehearted admiration, and I enjoy him as a great work of art.

I have often and often felt that there was something about genuine joy in things that transcended the person who partook in it, that it was parallel to the Catholic belief in the treasures of merit accumulated by the saints on which less well-endowed Christians could draw in their need. Perhaps I am too complacent in hoping that a life like mine has somehow contributed—not so much through what I spoke or published, but in some mystic way—to the capacity for joy of the rest of mankind.

It is easy now to live in ecstasy. I dare confess that at times I feel as if I understood the ecstasy of Saint Francis as painted in Sassetta's great triptych or better still of the lost Bellini Christ, white-robed and manly, radiant in the joy of sun and sky and earth that he is at one with, known to us in a mediocre copy by Previtali (now at the Brera in Milan).

All ambition spent, I have no envy or jealousy left in me to intervene between me and what contemporaries are doing and being and to blind me to their worth. I can appreciate any and every gift to the point of worship and I discover in most creative things done nowadays far more to admire and to enjoy than ever before. I only wish I had the will to passivity becoming to my age.

At times I feel like many a one in Nazi-haunted Europe who always had a bag ready, in case the Gestapo or its local jackals came to carry him off. I am packed and, with Landor, "ready to depart," but not peppering to do so.

All I ask of these years left me is to keep my perception and judgement, to be supplied with creature comforts and to go on taking interest in events, enjoying books, enjoying art and music, but above all enjoying nature and people.

So with La Fontaine in his "Invocation" I can intone:

Volupté, Volupté, qui fus jadis maîtresse
Du plus bel esprit de la Grèce,
Ne me dédaigne pas, viens-t'en loger chez moi;
Tu n'y seras pas sans emploi:
J'aime le jeu, l'amour, les livres, la musique,
La ville et la campagne, enfin tout; il n'est rien
Qui ne me soit souverain bien
Jusqu'au sombre plaisir d'un cœur mélancolique.
Viens donc; et de ce bien, ô douce Volupté,
Veux-tu savoir au vrai la mesure certaine?
Il m'en faut tout au moins un siècle bien compté;
Car trente ans, ce n'est pas la peine.

Sir Edward Marsh, who has so miraculously Englished La Fontaine's *Fables,* has translated the above verses as follows:

Delight! Delight! who mistress wert of yore
To the most rarest wit Greece ever bore,
Disdain me not! Come down with me to dwell;
I warrant I'll employ thee well.
Music I love, and books and all sweet folly,

The town, the country, love and cards and
wine,
All these ensky me—everything, in fine,
Ev'n to the sombre bliss of musing mel-
ancholy.
Come, then! and shall I tell thee, dear
Delight,
Of this our joy the measure true?
A century at least we'ld claim of right,
For thirty years were all too few.

CASA AL DONO, VALLOMBROSA.
August 1945